A Victorian

Sea Adventure

The Final Voyage of the Clipper Ship *Teviotdale* in 1876

A true account of a frightening shipwreck and human survival from Able Seaman George Jenkins and his shipmates.

by George Jenkins

Preface by Stuart McEwen Jenkins
Introduction and Editing by Carol McNeill
Additional Research by Robert Owen Hughes

A Victorian Sea Adventure
The Final Voyage of the Clipper Ship *Teviotdale* in 1876

by

George Jenkins

ISBN: 978-1-9160602-1-0

Copy edited by Ian Large

Cover design by Jag Lall

This book is produced by Teviotdale 60444 in conjunction with **WRITERSWORLD**, and is produced entirely in the UK. It is available to order from most bookshops in the United Kingdom, and is also globally available via UK based Internet book retailers.

WRITERSWORLD
2 Bear Close Flats, Bear Close, Woodstock
Oxfordshire, OX20 1JX, England
☎ 01993 812500
☎ +44 1993 812500

www.writersworld.co.uk

The text pages of this book are produced via an independent certification process that ensures the trees from which the paper is produced come from well managed sources that exclude the risk of using illegally logged timber while leaving options to use post-consumer recycled paper as well.

The Captain of the Teviotdale

I brought the "Teviotdale" in
On the evening tide
Having sailed
The oceans wide
Too late now
To begin discharging
Start first thing
In the early morning
Cannot let the crew ashore
They'd get drunk
And good for nothing
But after unloading
They'll be free
Not badly paid
For their days at sea
We lost no men
Thank God, I say
We struck fierce gales
On many a day
But the crew stood fast
And battened down
It's sad to see
A good man drown
I'll go now
And finish the log
It's overcast
And it looks like fog
But that's no concern to me
We are safely home
To bonnie Dundee

William Precey

Contents

Preface

This is a true account of the final voyage of the sailing ship *Teviotdale* in 1876. It was written by my grandfather, George Jenkins, and given as a lecture at a public meeting in the Tullibody Institute in 1909, Tullibody being a small town situated between Stirling and Alloa in Scotland. The lecture may have been given only once.

At the time of writing, George Jenkins was the Customs Superintendent for the Port of Alloa. He wrote two lecture introductions and was obviously quite nervous at the thought of giving a talk in front of an audience. I have recorded both introductions here, because they give an insight into his motivation to sit down and write down 37 pages, in beautiful copper plate, his recollections of this fateful voyage 33 years after the event.

An extract of George Jenkins' lecture introductory script.
"I can assure you..."

The lecture text has been edited quite comprehensively because my grandfather only wrote the lecture notes for his own benefit, not thinking that anyone would take much interest in them over 100 years later. Some of the language has been changed from the broad Scots and some words have been changed to be more politically correct for this day and age.

The story is historically significant and presents a snapshot of life at sea for a young seaman in mid-Victorian times, when British influence was at its zenith and many ships were sailing between the UK and India.

It is interesting to note that the *London Times* reported, under the title 'The Cruel Sea', on 16th August 2002 that "according to an Oxford University study, Trawler-men are 50 times more likely to be killed at work than the average, and Merchant seamen are 25 times more likely to be killed." Bearing in mind the marine navigational aids and rescue means available now, one has to appreciate just how dangerous life on a clipper ship was in Victorian times. George Jenkins lost his father and two brothers in shipping accidents and obviously considered that he had been lucky to have survived his 12 years spent at sea.

The preparation of this text has aroused a great interest in me and others to research the voyage of the *Teviotdale* further, to find out more about the crew of 27 that put to sea on that fateful voyage in 1876 and locate any of their descendants. In particular, poor Daly, who obviously suffered from a form of epilepsy, and the Mate who died and was buried at sea.

Stuart McEwen Jenkins
Bognor Regis
West Sussex
England

Background

George Jenkins was born in 1856 in the Royal Burgh of Perth, Tayside, now Perth and Kinross. His father was also a seaman; so it was probably inevitable that he – like countless others in Perth and the surrounding areas – would start off his working life by going to sea. His two brothers also were sailors, and sadly, along with his father (also named George Jenkins), all were lost in shipping accidents: his father drowned when the SS *Dalhousie* foundered on the bar of the River Tay in 1864 with all hands lost; his eldest brother fell from a large sailing ship on her homeward passage from Colombo to London in a strong gale off the Cape of Good Hope; and his younger brother, on the crew of a steam ship, died when his ship was lost in a gale in the Bay of Biscay.

The family tragedies, however, did not deter George from going to sea himself, and in 1876 he signed on as a crew member of the clipper *Teviotdale*, a fully-rigged ship built at Barclay Curle's yard in Glasgow and launched seven years previously. She left Dundee's Camperdown Dock on 26th July with a cargo of 1,790 tonnes of coal bound for Bombay. No doubt he assumed it would be an arduous but necessary voyage; in point of fact it was anything but, and as he described fully in 1909 in a talk given on his return, he and his shipmates were very fortunate to survive a disastrous fire on board ship. The crew had to take to three small open boats, navigating the vast expanse of the Indian Ocean until they landed on the tiny island of Diego Garcia in the Chagos Archipelago.

Thirty-three years later, when he was the Customs Superintendent of the Port of Alloa, he gave a lecture covering his recollections of this eventful voyage in the Public Hall situated in nearby Tullibody.

George's hand-written notes for his lecture, all 37 pages of them, came into my father's possession to reside in his bureau from the 1930s, when my family lived in Hoddesdon, Hertfordshire, to survive the Second World War, the Battle of Britain, the bombing raids, the V1 doodlebugs flying overhead and the V2 rockets, until 2004 when I took it into my head to type the story into my computer – which brought the story to life.

The lantern slides that George refers to in his narrative to illustrate his story were also stored in this bureau drawer and, unfortunately, these became lost when my family moved from Hoddesdon to Barnham, near Bognor Regis, West Sussex in 1955.

Hence my decision to commission a series of paintings and sketches of the clipper ship *Teviotdale* to represent these lantern slides.

The Custom House in Mid Quality Street, c.1904.
© Dysart Trust

Having survived that disastrous voyage, George carried on with his seafaring life, finishing up in 1884 when he entered the Customs Service. George had married Elizabeth McEwan on 2nd Feb 1880 in Dundee and sometime during 1881 Elizabeth gave birth to their first child, a daughter whom they named Georgina. Records from a local newspaper at the time show another daughter being born on 17th May 1885 at 37 Gellatly Street, Dundee, she was named Grace.

By 1890 when George was 34, he was a Customs Officer in Dundee, and over the years he moved up the Customs Services ladder to be appointed Principal Customs Officer at the small coal exporting port of Dysart, located on the south-east coast of the Firth of Forth estuary between Kirkcaldy and West Wemyss in Fife. Dysart is now considered to be a suburb of Kirkcaldy, once being part of a wider estate owned by the St Clair or Sinclair family.

Family life in Fife progressed with George working from the Custom House shop front in Dysart's Mid Quality Street; some members of the Jenkins family can be seen at the windows above the Mercantile Marine Office. In 1904, George was promoted from Principal Officer to Superintendent, having served for eight years. At the same time, the staff was increased by the addition of a second officer Mr John Hill, who came from Burntisland. In the photograph of the Customs House in Mid Quality Street, c.1904, George is on the left. Later on, the family moved to a house in the Pan Ha' (Hie-Gait), virtually situated on the estuary beach.

The author at the corner of the house in the Pan Ha'.

By 1909, George was Customs Superintendent for the Port of Alloa, when he gave a full account of his eventful *Teviotdale* voyage in a lecture at a public meeting in Tullibody, and his notes, carefully preserved by his son Charles Henry Ward Jenkins, for the lecture, form the main part of this book.

Stuart McEwen Jenkins, 2019.

𝔇𝔢𝔡𝔦𝔠𝔞𝔱𝔦𝔬𝔫𝔰

Walker / Jenkins Families Dedication

The *Teviotdale* story is dedicated to the memory of members of my family who endured the effects of the heredity disease, Limb Girdle Muscular Dystrophy.

To my maternal grandfather Walker, who suffered from it late in life, not knowing the nature of his disability. Grandfather Walker died sometime during the 1940s, he was in his early seventies when he passed away.

To Grandfather Walker's daughter, my mother, Ethel Victoria Jenkins, who began to suffer from the effects of Muscular Dystrophy in her late thirties. Ethel Jenkins found that she had increasing difficulty in walking; at the time she called it her 'Creeping Paralysis'. Ethel lived to the age of 84; in her later years confined to a wheelchair, lovingly looked after by my sister, Margaret Grace Jenkins.

To my brother, Henry Jenkins. In the case of Henry, Muscular Dystrophy began to take its toll in his late teens and early twenties. Henry emigrated to New Zealand and it was only here, and due to his increasing weakness and walking difficulty, that he was diagnosed as suffering from the rare heredity disease of Muscular Dystrophy. It was at this time that we realised that my mother, Ethel, was also suffering from the same condition.

Henry Jenkins came back to the United Kingdom in 1953 to have the diagnoses confirmed. Henry lived to the age of 71, unable to cope with the condition and its complications and, with the help of his wife Sybille, they both committed suicide in 1999.

To my elder sister, Margaret Grace Jenkins, born in 1923. Margaret began to suffer from the effects of Muscular Dystrophy in her late seventies, and continued to suffer until her death at the age of 89 in 2012.

14

In the case of my other brother, Alexander Jenkins, and myself, Stuart McEwen Jenkins, we have been lucky. However, in my case I was advised at the time of my marriage that I had a one-in-four chance of passing the disease on to any of my children. As a result, my wife Juliet and I decided to adopt. We now have the most wonderful daughter, Melanie Grace, who was born on 2nd August 1968. Although grown up now and having left home, we are both extremely proud of her achievements.

And finally, to all seamen who have lost their lives at sea.

Michael Daly and Epilepsy

Having read through my grandfather's narrative many times during the preparation of this book, I now realise that his memories of the incidents relating to Daly, during the voyage, were somewhat unkind. As a young seaman he clearly did not have any sympathetic understanding of the condition relating to Daly's epilepsy or again as a Senior Customs Superintendent, some 33 years later, when he gave his Tullibody lecture.

However, in Victorian times, epilepsy was a little understood condition and grandfather cannot be blamed for his opinion because anyone with any such condition was generally considered to be mad. Also, it must be said that the Captain and his officers also had such opinions, making me think as to how Daly was managed – was he expected to climb up the ship's rigging on to the yard arms in all weathers to attend to the sails?

Michael Daly gave his place of birth as Cork in Ireland and his address as a lodging in Dundee. This makes me think that perhaps he had been rejected by his family.

I can only think that, perhaps, Daly did not understand that he was suffering from a medical condition when he was signed on as a crew member.

Daly's epilepsy is mentioned in the final official enquiry and report subsequently held in Mauritius.

My one and only personal experience with epilepsy occurred in the 1960s when I was employed as a senior mechanical engineer at the GEC Applied Electronics Laboratories in Portsmouth. We had a progress chaser working with us, his name was Eric Peters and his job, which he did very well, was to coordinate all associated activities relating to the project.

We usually conducted these meetings early in the morning, and on one such occasion Eric was sitting with my group when he had an epileptic seizure. His arms and legs shot out in front of him; his eyes rolled to show the whites and he rolled on to the floor and I found this very frightening. One of my colleagues said Eric had had one of his turns and called for the nurse to come. He was quite matter of fact about this, having had to cope with Eric having a fit before. The nurse duly came with a trolley and wheeled Eric away. In the afternoon Eric appeared again quite unconcerned, carrying on as usual.

Some weeks later Eric appeared with his face badly bruised with his arm in a sling and limping badly, trying to carry on as usual. I was informed that when going home after work he had fallen from top to bottom on the footbridge steps at the nearby Hilsea railway station. Shortly afterwards Eric disappeared from the scene and I never received any further news of him.

Even today, epilepsy is a medical conundrum and a human tragedy.

About the Book

I first became aware of the handwritten manuscript recording my grandfather's memories of his epic voyage in the clipper ship *Teviotdale* in 1876 when I was a child during the years prior to World War 2. However, it was not until 2004 that I took a real interest in what has proved to be a remarkable true story.

This interest was sparked off by an invitation from a crew member taking part in one of the first Round the World yacht races, which was due to start from Portsmouth later in the year. A crew member had noticed my company's website advertising military combat identification and search and rescue beacons and, as a result, our UK sales agent and I were invited to visit Southampton Harbour to actually go on board one of these yachts to discuss their requirements.

One requirement was for a flashing rescue beacon which could be attached to a life jacket in case of 'man overboard' and the other was for a simple glow wand device for the crew to use when manning the yacht during pitch darkness without dazzling the helmsman during heavy seas. It was during this conversation that I began to think of what it would have been like for the crew of the *Teviotdale*, sailing under these self-same dangerous conditions in the southern Indian Ocean, also in pitch darkness.

As a result, I became very friendly with the crew members of this particular yacht and I was very happy to supply a number of our devices for the crew to test for us during their voyage round the world.

On the day they set sail from Gun Wharf Quay in Portsmouth I went to wish the crew of this yacht 'bon voyage' and I gave them a copy of my grandfather's handwritten narrative to take on board to sail around the world with them, in memory of my grandfather.

The Final Voyage – A Victorian Sea Adventure is the culmination of our research into the events surrounding the loss of the *Teviotdale*, and incorporates the full text of my grandfather's lecture on the clipper ship's fateful voyage. I hope it will be of interest to all those with an interest in the sea and conditions on board such ships from a bygone era.

About the Author

When Stuart McEwen Jenkins was born in 1935 his family had moved to be near London so that his father could operate a haulage company, called Jenkins Express Removals, one of the first long-distance removals businesses to operate in the UK; his brother, James was in charge of the company's Scottish office in Glasgow.

This was the time of the 1930s Depression and there was great demand for people to move house from one end of the country to the other. Consequently, due to the demand of the service from their business, Stuart's family were comparatively well off, with the result that his father, a natural born engineer, could take up his interest in boats.

In about 1938 he bought a second-hand lifeboat from a yard in Southampton; he named the boat the *Margaret*. Stuart's father had it converted into a comfortable 6-berth motor cruiser fitted with a petrol engine he had converted for marine use in his home garage workshop. Stuart has a childhood memory of him testing this engine with it spewing out coolant water on to the garage forecourt. He sailed the *Margaret* along the Channel coast to Fambridge-on-Crouch in Essex and he remembers his family having a good time sailing up and down the estuary on weekends.

During the war years Stuart's father became a volunteer member of the Admiralty Small Boat Pool, which was vital in the success of the D-Day landings, from where he brought home a shell casing that had been fired during the Normandy landings. When he died in 1973 the base of this casing was incorporated into a memorial at the family grave site in Dysart Cemetery.

During the periods that his father spent at home he began to teach Stuart the basics of engineering which has stood him in good stead for all his life. In 1949 he gained a place at the Northampton Polytechnic Secondary Technical School in London for a 3-year engineering course followed by a further 3 years at the National College of Horology (NCH) where he obtained an Honours Diploma.

At the age of 19, Stuart became a graduate apprentice at Smiths Aircraft Instruments based in Cheltenham. During this time he studied for a National Certificate in Engineering with Endorsements and later became a Chartered Engineer (CEng).

National Service then followed for two years during which he was based at the Proof and Experimental Establishment on Foulness Island where he had a great opportunity to make use of his engineering skills.

After National Service Stuart took a job with the Plessey company based in Havant, Hampshire, busy at the time making parts for radios and after a short time he moved on to their nearby Titchfield plant. In 1963, he took up a Senior Mechanical Engineer position with the GEC company based in Portsmouth and spent six years working on very interesting projects.

In 1969, Stuart became a project manager at the newly-established De la Rue Instruments factory in Portsmouth to develop cash dispensing machines. He spent 16 years with this company and was fortunate to work, mainly, with the NCR and Diebold companies based in the USA, and some European companies. During this period he was responsible for the multi-denomination cash dispenser design which has been incorporated in 'all' ATMs in use up to this day.

In 1985, Stuart started his own business ventures, starting with the design of a dot matrix destination blind for buses and went on to form a company designing combat identification 'CID' devices for military use. In all, Stuart has accumulated some 41 patents during his career.

Chapter One

The Teviotdale Story –
Crew List and Mission Statement

The mission of the *Teviotdale* in the July of 1876 was to deliver 1,790 tons of Scotch coals to Bombay in India. At the time the *Teviotdale* sailed from Dundee, Scotland, a pre-planned mission statement of every sea voyage was required. This was known as the Agreement and Account of Crew, and was laid out in a series of forms held together as an official document and lodged with the Registrar General of Seamen at the Mercantile Marine Office, Board of Trade.

Below is an extract of some of the crew members (taken from Agreement & Account of Crew No. 26762, 3rd August 1876, courtesy of The National Maritime Museum, London):

> **Master**: Robert Jones, 38, of Bangor. Cert no. 93738.
> **Mate**: John Miller, 41, of Dundee. Cert no. 85193.
> **2nd Mate**: George Symons, 38, of Dundee. Cert no. 25262.
> **Carpenter**: Henry Owen, 23, of Bangor.
> **Sailmaker**: James Hawkset, 36, of Glasgow.
> **Steward**: James Beattie, 62, of Dundee.
> **Cook**: Albert Cropkey, 37, of Rye.

> *and amongst the remainder of the sailors were:*

> **AB** (Able-bodied seaman): George Jenkins, 20, of Perth.
> **AB**: Michael Daly, 30, of Cork.

The above men, along with 21 other able-bodied seamen on board, including with Master and all crew, made a total of 30 at the time of sailing. Note that at the time of abandoning the ship in the Indian Ocean there were only 27 crew listed, including the Master, divided equally between the three longboats, each having nine on board.

From the extensive records of the National Archives, National Maritime Museum and the various other official bodies that look after the collections of the National Archives, we have researched and extracted numerous files of historical relevance to the *Teviotdale*, its Masters and Mates, crew details and mission statement. The transcribed extract below gives details of the *Teviotdale's* final mission.

Agreement and Account of Crew (Foreign-Going* Ship)

The several persons whose names are hereto subscribed, and whose descriptions are contained on the other side or sides, and of whom _____ are engaged as Sailors and hereby agree to serve on the said Ship, in the several capacities expressed against their respective Names, on a Voyage from:

> *the Tay to Bombay and/or any ports or places in the East Indies, China, Arabian and Eastern Seas, West Indies, Atlantic, Pacific and Indian Oceans, North and South America and/or, United States of America, to and fro as circumstances permit for a period not exceeding three years and back to final port of discharge in the United Kingdom or on the Continent of Europe ~ with power to call at any place for orders. ~*

The ship shall be deemed fully manned with 22 hands all told. ~

In Witness whereof the said parties have subscribed their Names on the other side or sides hereof on the days against the respective Signatures mentioned.

Signed by: Robert Jones Master on the 21st day of July 1876

Author's note: Voyages to the Islands of Guernsey, Jersey, Sark, Alderney, Man, and the European coast between Brest in Normandy, France to the Elbe estuary, Hamburg, Germany were not considered foreign-going.

Credit: National Maritime Museum, London.

Name of

PARTICULARS OF ENGAGEMENT.

Reference No.	SIGNATURES OF CREW.	Age.	Town or County where born.	If in the Navy, No. of Commission or R.V.S.	Ship in which he last served. State Name and Official No. or Port she belonged to.	Year.	Date.	Place.	In what Capacity engaged.	Time at which he is to be on board.
1	Robert Jones *(Master to sign first.)*	38	Bangor		Teviotdale				9373 Master	
2	John Miller	40	Dundee		Victory Egm	1876	24/7/76	D[undee]	8519 Mate 2526	24th 8 am
3	George Symons	38	do		Dunedin Egm	do	do	do	2nd Mate	do
4	Henry Owen	23	Bangor		Macedon Egm	do	do	do	Carpenter	do
5	James Harkess	36	Glasgow		Christy McGlone Egm	July 25	do	Sailmaker	on board
6	James Boothie	62	Dundee		Luther Egm	1876	24/7/76	Dundee	Steward	24 Egm
7	Albert Crospky	27	Rye		Lochee Egm	1876	24/7/76	Dundee	Cook	24 Egm 9 am
8	Robert × Kirkpatrick		Newcastle		Harmony Egm	do	do	do	AB	do
9	Francis Spalding	19	Liverpool		Teviotdale Egm	do	do	do	AB	do
10	Thomas × Skally	23	Ireland		do	do	do	do	AB	do
11	William Keay	20	Dundee		Greenock Egm	do	do	do	AB	do
12	George Hay	35	St Helens		Resine Leon	do	do	do	AB	do
13	George Kendrew	32	Manchester		do	do	do	do	AB	do
14	John Brown	28	Glasgow		Circassian Quebec	do	do	do	AB	do
15	Joseph Baker	42	Sunderland		Aldersons Ebm	do	do	do	AB	do
16	James McDoig	18	Dundee		First Ship		do	do	Boy	do
17	George Robertson	16	do		do		do	do	Boy	do
18	Charles McWalter	17	Manchester		do		do	do	Boy	do
19	Alex Fletcher	24	Dundee	289	Sisters		do	do	AB	do
20	George Jenkins	21	Perth	5220	Shields do		do	do	AB	do

Amount of Wages per Week, Calendar Month, Run, or Voyage.	Amount of Wages advanced on Entry.	Amount of Weekly or Monthly Allotment.	Signature or Initials of Superintendent, Consul, or Officer of Customs.	ADDRESS OF MASTER OR CREW.
			Athytock	3 Britannia Terrace, Anytown
8	8	4	*Athytock*	48 Princes Street
5	5	2 10	*JW*	Brown St Bro Ferry
6 10	6 10		*JW*	32 Castle Street
5	5	2 10	*JW*	61 Henstock Paisley Road Glasgow
4 10	4 10	2 5	*JW*	138 Perth Road
4 4	4 4	2 2	*JW*	Whartton Bank Lochee
3 5	3 5	1 12 6	*JW*	do
3 5	3 5		*JW*	do
3 5	3 5	1 12 6	*JW*	St Mary Lane Lochee
3 5	3 5	1 12 6	*JW*	38 South Wellington St
3 5	3 5		*JW*	24 Gillatly St
3 6	3 5		*JW*	do
3 5	3 5		*JW*	42 Crofts Lane
3 5	3 5		*JW*	12 Castle St
4 5			*JW*	Monifieth
5			*JW*	17 Roberton St
15	15		*JW*	111 Upper Pleasance
3 5	3 5	15	*JW*	Dalfield Walk
3 5	3 5		*JW*	55 King Street

As can be seen from the Agreement here, the ship's Master had the power and authority to navigate the East Indies, China, Arabian and Eastern Seas, West Indies, Atlantic, Pacific and Indian Oceans, North and South America and/or, United States of America, for up to three years. The voyage was of course planned to return to Britain, but owing to the nature of sailing in the 19th century, it was not guaranteed. A sailor may well find himself landed at a European port, or worse still, a port much further afield as was the case with the Master and crew of the *Teviotdale*.

The Teviotdale Story

Introduction

Public Hall Lecture, Tullibody, 1909

Mr Chairman, Ladies and Gentlemen,

I can assure you it gives me the greatest of pleasure to come here to Tullibody[1] and tell you my sea story. I have had the pleasure of being present at two or three of your lectures this session, and I have enjoyed them very much. In my attendance at them, I have paid particular attention to the very quiet, attentive and appreciative audiences that have attended.

Lime-Light Lecture and Concert.

A lime-light lecture and concert in aid of the funds of the County Hospital was given in the Museum Hall on Thursday evening. Provost Calder presided, and the Hall was filled to its utmost capacity. The Provost briefly introduced the lecturer, Mr George Jenkins of H.M. Customs, Alloa, whose subject was "Reminiscences of Sea Life." Mr Jenkins throughout his lecture, lasting over an hour, sustained the appreciative attention of the audience. The lecture consisted of a description of a voyage from Dundee to Bombay in the sailing ship "Teviotdale." At the outset the lecturer described the system of crimping in vogue thirty years ago whereby

Now, I trust you do not expect of me that I am to excel, or come up to the standard of the previous lectures. But my subject is new, for what people are clamouring for is for

---

[1] *The town of Tullibody underwent major redevelopment during the 20th century and little of the original town remains.*

26

something new, and that will perhaps, make up for some of the deficiency and fill the gap. Another point, the subject is from my own personal experience and, also from my own pen.

Public Hall, Tullibody, c.1909.
This is the building where George Jenkins gave his lecture.

The pictures that I have, in connection with this lecture and very good pictures they are; have been accurately drawn to my description, to illustrate this rather vivid incident in a memorable voyage. They have been drawn by one of our own men: Mr. A R Blair. However, the picture that I want you to pay particular attention to tonight is the one I am about to lay before you; I mean the picture of a sailor's life at sea. Therefore I hope that none of you will become seasick before I have finished.

George Jenkins, Tullibody, 17th December 1909.

2ⁿᵈ or Alternative Introduction²

Mr Chairman, Ladies and Gentlemen,

I should like to mention, before beginning, that the writing of the story of this particular voyage is not a new idea of mine. It has been my ambition for years, but it was only lately, in fact since I came to Alloa, that I have had the opportunity to obtain the four pictures, which have been accurately drawn to my description, to illustrate some of the rather vivid incidents in a memorable voyage. They have been drawn by one of our own men, Mr Blair, and I can assure you that they are very good pictures indeed.

Customs House Officers, Tullibody. Taken in the early 1900s, possibly around 1909 at the time of his lecture. George Jenkins is 3ʳᵈ from left.

Photo from Jenkins family archives.

² *The 2ⁿᵈ or alternative introduction is one that was found folded inside the booklet where George Jenkins had written his notes for the talk all those years ago. Both introductions were written in his handwriting and dated 17ᵗʰ December 1909.*

28

Ladies and Gentlemen,

I should like to mention before beginning that the writing of the story of this particular voyage is not a new idea of mine, it has been my ambition for years, but, it was only lately, in fact since I came to Alloa that I have had the opportunity to get the four pictures which have been accurately drawn to my description, to illustrate this rather vivid incident in a memorable voyage. They have been drawn by one of our own men, Mr Blair. And I can assure you, to my idea at least, they are very good pictures. While I was in London last summer on holiday I had them photographed and the lantern plates made from them, that I am to throw on the screen tonight. As this is my first attempt of anything of this kind, should any little hitch occur which I will do my best to avoid, I trust you will look over it. So with your kind attention I will now endeavour to lay before you, the picture, of a sailors life at Sea.

While I was in London last summer on holiday, I had them photographed to create the lantern plates that I am going to throw on to the screen tonight.

As this is my first attempt of anything of this kind, if any little hitch should occur, which I will do my best to avoid, I trust you will overlook it. So, with your kind attention I will endeavour to lay before you the picture of a sailor's life at sea.

George Jenkins, Tullibody, 17th December 1909.

George Jenkins c.1884, aged about 28.

Photo from Jenkins family archives.

At this time George lived in Dundee and can be seen here in his Customs House uniform. Shortly after this photograph of George was taken, his wife Elizabeth gave birth to their second baby, named Grace, who was born on 17th May 1885 at 37 Gellatly Street, Dundee.

Foreword

Most people have read or sung of the jolly tars that man our navy and mercantile vessels, but few landsmen have any real idea of what life at sea means. There is no doubt that the sea exercises a fascination to most young lads, but those who choose the sea as their profession soon learn the sterner side of the jolly life of the sailor. The fact that sailors have innumerable perils and dangers, even staring death in the face when they are battling with the storms they have to encounter, develops a stoutness of heart or a devil-may-care attitude that makes them heroes in young lads' eyes. And among the older people, the proverbial cheeriness of Jack ashore makes them more kindly and forgiving of his faults, as they know he has to face so many dangers for our benefit and welfare.

Very often the love of the sea seems to run in families and, although some members of the family are drowned at sea, it does not deter the others from following the same profession.

In my own case, although my own father was drowned through the foundering of the SS *Dalhousie* on the bar of the Tay in 1864, when all hands perished, it did not keep me from taking to a sea life. Both of my brothers were subsequently drowned at sea; my eldest brother fell overboard from a large sailing ship on her homeward passage from Colombo to London at three o'clock in the morning, with the vessel running before a strong gale off the Cape of Good Hope. There is not much chance for you if you should slip and fall. My other brother, who was younger than me, died when a steam ship was supposed to have foundered in a gale in the Bay of Biscay, with all hands lost.

For myself, I have been more fortunate, for during my twelve years of seafaring life, before I entered the service of His Majesty's Customs, I have mostly been on long voyages, in steam and sailing vessels; during the earlier part sailing vessels, and the latter part steam, but I finished up in a sailing ship in 1884, after which I entered the Customs Service.

My purpose tonight is to give you a short sketch of one of my escapes on a voyage from Dundee in Scotland to Bombay, India.[3] I was signed to the sailing ship *Teviotdale* of Glasgow, in 1876 when I had just turned 20 years of age, and I hope that this account may give you some idea, from a sailor's point of view, of some of the incidents that may happen on a voyage.

---

[3] *Bombay is now called Mumbai and is on the Arabian Sea coast of India.*

The Clipper Ship *Teviotdale*

The Clipper Ship Teviotdale in 1876 - 'Scudding Along' in the English Channel.

On Teviotdale's penultimate voyage home, she was sighted passing Dover and reported safe.

The *Teviotdale* was a fine clipper ship; fully rigged, 1,259 registered tons and built at Glasgow some three or four years previously.[4] The crew, as is often the case, was composed of Scots, English, Irish and

---

[4] *From the ship's register, now held in The London Maritime Museum, Greenwich, it was recorded that the Teviotdale was officially launched in 1869; therefore it can be seen the ship was seven years old.*

Welshmen, with a foreigner or two thrown in. The Master, a genial kind-hearted man, was a Welshman, the Mate was from Dundee and the Second Mate, Broughty Ferry. In the forecastle[5] we were, of course, a well-mixed lot; amongst us was a very tall thin Irishman called Daly whom we soon came to regard as a fit subject for an asylum rather than as a sailor on board a ship.

Camperdown Dock 2016.
Photo © 2016 Robert Hughes

---

[5] *The forecastle is the forward part of a ship below the deck. Traditionally used as the crew's living quarters.*

Anchored In the Tay

It was on the afternoon of 26th of July 1876 when the *Teviotdale*, with a cargo of about eighteen hundred (1,800) tons of coal, left the Camperdown Dock, Dundee, but as our crew had not been properly completed, we anchored in the river till the following day. At that time, large seaports were infected with Crimps and Boarding Masters, commonly called Hand Sharks, all eager to rob poor Jack of his hard-earned money.

When there was a scarcity of seamen at the port, Captains were obliged to apply to these Hand Sharks to obtain men for them and, if they could not get sailors, they would pick up anything in the way of men, no matter what trade, profession or otherwise, give him a few drinks of firewater to inflate his courage, put a blue sailor's cap on him, and represent him to the Skipper as a fully-fledged sailor. The men being drunk, the Skipper would ask no questions, but the Crimp had to see they were put safely on board. This having been accomplished, the Crimp would receive his fee which generally consisted of an advance note for a month's wages for each of the men he put on board. This advance note was payable three days after the ship had sailed and only on consideration that the men were still on board the ship. But the Crimp would look pretty sharp that he did not take his men on board till they were well charged with firewater and the ship about ready to sail, and before they were properly sober they were out at sea. Due to present severe restrictions and penalties the Board of Trade inflicts on Crimps, they are almost a thing of the past. Although this was bad in Britain, it was ten times worse at some American ports. It is said that at San Francisco a boarding master put a dead man on board a ship at the time of sailing, receiving a month's advance for him, and told the Captain that he was only drunk and would prove himself a good man when he woke up.

Reverting back to that night, lying in the river, about midnight a boat came alongside with a boarding master and two sailors to complete our crew. Well, they appeared to be sailors; they had blue jerseys and sailor caps on. But to our dismay they turned out to be two riveters who had tramped from Glasgow and had only arrived in the town late in the evening, weary and footsore from their long walk, and glad to meet anyone when they fell into the Crimp's snare. He soon livened them up with a few drinks, faked (dressed) them up with the blue jerseys, soon had them in his boat and off to the ship; got the usual fee, of course, and left them to their fate. They began to ask questions that rather nonplussed the sailors. There was a pump near the forecastle for pumping sea water used for washing down decks and when one of them said there must be a mighty lot of fresh water down the holds that we could keep pumping so long, that told us that our new friends, despite their sailor rig, knew nothing about the ship or the sea. However, they had signed articles as able seamen and would have to be made sailors somehow or other.

The Voyage Begins

With over twenty sails to look after, the able seaman was kept busy aloft.

A tough job fixing the sail to the jackstay on board Teviotdale in 1876.

The next morning, the tugboat with the pilot came alongside; we weighed anchor and were towed out as far as the Bellrock [known as Bell Rock today]. A few sails were set and we parted company with the tugboat and pilot. All sail was then set, and with a gentle easterly breeze our eventful voyage had now fairly begun.

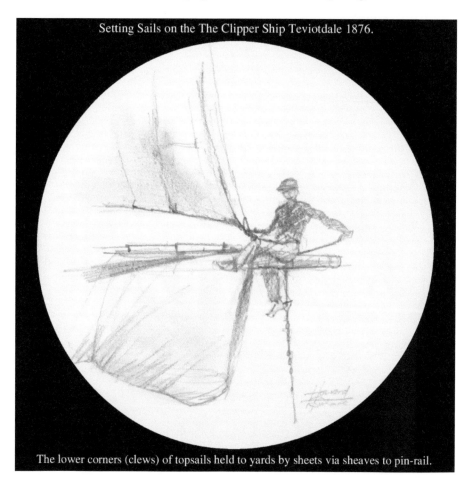

Setting Sails on the The Clipper Ship Teviotdale 1876.

The lower corners (clews) of topsails held to yards by sheets via sheaves to pin-rail.

It is customary, after the decks are cleared with anchors and everything moveable secured, for the Officers to choose their Watches. The Mate has the Port Watch and the Second Mate the Starboard Watch. The crew is mustered on the quarterdeck and the First Mate has the first pick, then the Second Mate chooses a man and so on, until the Watches are completed. The Mate's first choice fell on Daly as he was such a tall strapping fellow. But we will find as we get further on, he rued his choice.

Our first experience with Daly occurred the night we sailed. We were sailing along the Aberdeenshire coast between 9 and 10pm with a fine breeze on our starboard beam, when the lookout man reported a number of bright lights right ahead. These proved to be the lights of fishing vessels hanging on their nets, and the noise the fishermen made shouting at us to keep clear of their nets brought the whole of the watch onto the forecastle head to see what was the matter. The Second Mate was also on the forecastle head shouting to the helmsman to keep the ship away so as to clear the fishing vessels and nets. Suddenly, a most unearthly yell was heard from the forecastle below.

After a second or two, a rush was made to see what had happened. Daly was discovered on top of the cable chains with his face terribly cut and bleeding and in a fit. He had jumped out of the top bunk when he took the fit. After getting him out of the fit and his wounds dressed, it was considered safer to put him in the lower bunk. And we laced the front of the bunk into a network to keep him in.

Shortly after this incident when things had quietened down, I went into the forecastle as it was our watch below. I can assure you that I did not feel very comfortable, especially having to sleep on the same side of the forecastle as Daly, even for only that night, bearing in mind that one of our shipmates had previously assured us that Daly had once been in a mad house which made it even worse; however, we had to make the best of it.

I was sitting filling my pipe to have a smoke, when I heard a rustle from Daly's bunk. Looking forward I saw Daly sitting up and his eyes were glaring and rolling about, when he suddenly fixed them on me. The front of his bunk was all laced, but the end through which he was looking was not. All kinds of thoughts flashed through my head at that moment. What if he should spring out at me? I felt my hair beginning to stand on end and I was ready to make a bolt for the forecastle door should he make another move, when he suddenly let out an unearthly yell and went into another fit. After this, I could not think of sleeping on the same side as Daly, even for that night. So I resolved to remove my goods and chattels to the other side there and then.

I get along with many different kinds of men but I did not look forward to enjoying the voyage for so many months with a madman on board. However, a sailor is not like a landsman, he cannot give into his feelings and chuck in his job when things become uncomfortable; he has just to suffer it out. As the old saying has it: "Growl (complain) you may, but go you must." There is no doubt that it is all this that Jack has to put up with plus being compelled to face the inevitable that makes him so hardy and determined to look at the brightest side of everything.

In the Doldrums

After passing the Pentland Firth into the North Atlantic we catch the North East trade winds, which carry us South almost to the Equator. Here we get into what are called the Doldrums. In this zone, in the tropics, you are between the regions of the North East and South East trade winds, and they are well named the Doldrums, for they will give you the dumps before you get out of them. First you may get a calm, then perhaps heavy squalls and then variable winds. In fact, the wind will shift about right round the compass. It is then that many a growl (complaint) comes from the sailors because of the continual hauling round of the yards. No sooner do you have them round to the wind, when the wind shifts in the opposite direction and round they have to go again and so it is repeated, making the progress of the ship very slow, and I can assure you the sailors are pleased when they get clear of this region.

The Clipper Ship Teviotdale Becalmed in the Equitorial Dolrums in 1876, where the Northerly and Southerly Trade Winds meet between North America and Africa.

After catching the South East Trade winds our voyage proceeded favourably towards the Cape of Good Hope. But long before we reach that wild part, we prepare for the heavy weather that is generally experienced in that region of the globe. All the light weather sails are unbent and taken down, and the storm canvas is put up in their place. This entails a lot of work, and pretty hard work it is for, if any of you have noticed the very large sails on board these big vessels that trade to the East Indies, you will have some idea of the difficulty of taking all those sails down and bending on heavier ones in their place.

However, that is part of Jack's work and so, with many a growl and many a verse of a shanty, the work proceeds till our good ship is all dressed in her winter clothes. "But what of Daly?" you may ask? Oh well, we have all pretty well got used to him and his war dances, as we call them, with the exception of the Mate who never seemed to get used to him. But I was rather inclined to sympathize with the Mate, for it wasn't a very nice thing to have a madman come up on the poop deck where you had to keep your lonely midnight watch, and cut an acrobatic performance by yelling and tumbling somersaults in front of you. I didn't wonder at the Mate running down from the poop one night and crying out that for goodness sake, come and take Daly out of this and make sure he doesn't come up here anymore.

The Second Mate was made of different stuff; he seemed to see the humorous side and nothing pleased him better to see Daly in one of his war dances. He also was of a very tricky disposition; he could, and would, act Daly to a nicety. Both Daly and the Second Mate were about the same height and both wore long overcoats in the night time. One night, when the Second Mate was in one of his larking moods and we had just finished squaring the yards, he said, "What do you say, we will have a lark with Simpson." This was one of the riveters who was the lookout on top of the forecastle head. We were to stand back in the dark and see the fun of the Second Mate crawling gently up on to the forecastle to get in front of Simpson. He then let out one of Daly's war whoops and danced in front of him, and if it had not been that the Second Mate could keep his mirth in check no longer and gave the show away, I believe Simpson, the riveter, would have jumped overboard. So you can imagine his feelings when he found out it was only one of the Second Mate's larks.

As I have already said, we were drawing near, or may say rounding the Cape of Good Hope, or what we term running the Eastern Down. You very seldom round the 'Cape of Storms' as it is also commonly called, without

46

getting into strong North West Gales that will last for several days, and when a North West Gale is at its height, the sea rises higher here than in any part of the known world, sometimes being over 40 feet high.

The clipper ship Teviotdale, 'Running the Easting Down'.

Monstrous seas abound in the roaring forties around the Cape of Good Hope - 1876.

But looking up at these high seas from the ship's deck when the vessel is in the trough of the sea, it appears at least three times that height; in fact, so fearsome does it look that the man at the wheel is forbidden to look round at it for it appears as if the mountain of water that

follows a ship when she is running with the wind will topple down and completely bury the ship. As the wave approaches, the vessel's stern rises and rises till she is lifted right on top of the sea, but the tops of

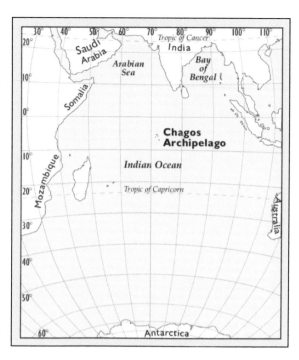

those giant waves, as they rush and curl along the vessel's side, will topple in at the waist of the ship, first on one side and then on the other, till the decks are filled and the good ship trembles and staggers, while the water pours in volumes out through the ports, the doors of which are lashed up to allow the water full scope to run off the deck. And as the burden of water clears off her decks, one feels the ship lifting and bounding forward again. To the sailor there is nothing very fearful about tons of water tumbling on board, so long as the vessel is running well before the wind, especially if everything holds well. But to passengers, or those who have not seen such sights before, it will try the stoutest hearts.

I remember, in another ship, when I was going round this Cape and we had thirty immigrants on board, all tradesmen from Glasgow, and we had the same weather I have just been describing. We were bound this time to Adelaide in Australia and it was rather amusing to us to see those big burly fellows; how white and scared they looked; they evidently thought it was about their last and that the end was not far off. I suppose about all their experience of the sea would be, "Doon the Watter" (a sail down the Clyde at the Glasgow Fair). What makes me introduce this other voyage is that there was a rather amusing episode that came under my own hearing that I have never forgotten. One night, the vessel was rolling a little heavier than usual and shipping a good deal of water on the decks. None of the immigrants would go to bed that night and I was standing at the hatchway, aft, that led to their quarters. I could see them gathered round their big lamp that hung in the centre, singing hymns most earnestly, when one of them, a big burly mason, came up the hatch to have a look to see if there was a ghost of a chance of escaping from Davy Jones's clutches. He asked some questions as to whether I thought she would weather this gale. Just at this time, a heavy sea toppled in on board and he said, "Oh my, just look at that," and down the hatch he went again. When he got down, I could see all the rest cluster round him asking, "How is she noo?" How is she looking noo?" And he said with great emphasis, "Oh boys she's settling doon fest, sing another hymn." But after we got into fine weather, very little hymn-singing was heard from their quarters.

They were something like the minister on a voyage who remonstrated with the Captain for allowing the sailors to swear too much. But when a gale sprang up, the minister was a bit frightened and asked the Captain if there was any danger. The Skipper, to have a hit back at the Parson, said that as long as he heard the forecastle sailors swearing, he could depend on it that everything was all right. Night came and things looked glummy (dangerous) to the minister and it is recorded that he was seen returning from the forecastle door where he had gone to listen and had heard some very tall swears, quite joyful and muttering to himself, "Thank God, the sailors are still swearing."

Fire

Well, after getting round the Cape, it was not long before we were into nice warm weather again. All the heavy weather canvas had been taken down and light sails had been put up in their place. We were now scudding along beautifully in the fine trade winds that are generally experienced in the Indian Ocean and making to cross the Equator for the second time.

On Monday morning, 2nd November 1876, my watch below was awakened by a lot of talking by the watch on deck who were gathered round the fore hatch. After giving my eyes a rub, the talking was still going on and through curiosity I jumped out of the bunk and came out to the hatch to see what it was all about. The cook says to me, "George, just put your head into that ventilator and have a sniff." I did so and got a very strong smell of gas. I said, "A strong smell of gas there, Cook." "Yes," he said, "you mark my word, this ship is on fire and if we are not out of here in 24 hours, I'm a Dutchman," a common expression on board ship, even though you belong to Tobermory.

I may mention our cook, only two voyages previous to this one, had been burned out of a vessel called the *St. Mungo* which had also left Dundee with a coal cargo. So he was considered an authority and, when he was so thoroughly convinced that the *Teviotdale* was on fire, you may guess how serious it made us all feel. For gales or hurricanes or wind or fogs, Jack is used to them and it does not put him much about. But his ship to be on fire, and nothing in sight but hundreds of miles of sea around him with the only means of escape a small boat, is a very serious dread for him, and he begins to realize that there is danger looming ahead.

But, I must revert back to the talking around the foresight (forecastle). It was about five in the morning and the Captain was asleep when the Mate went to inform him of what they had discovered and our strong suspicion that the ship was on fire. The Captain was immediately on foot and forward to the hatch to investigate and it was not long before he was convinced that there were good grounds for our suspicion. Well he says, "Boys we must do all we can to get at the seat of the fire," and gave the Mate his instructions to work the coals up from the fore hatch in baskets and put them in the forepeak. This was carried on for a short time, when it was considered better and quicker to dump the coal overboard. Very little smoke was seen but the gas fumes were getting stronger and stronger every minute, causing those in the hold shovelling, to complain of severe headaches. At 8am the watch was relieved and the starboard watch went at it with a will, working very hard, in very trying circumstances under a tropical sun, up until noon. The smoke and gas was now increasing at an alarming rate. The Captain had ascertained the position of the ship and found that the nearest land was the island of Diego Garcia, lying about E by N and distance about 250 miles. The ship was now close hauled to the wind and steering as near as possible to the course for that island.

After dinner, all hands were called on deck. One watch was set to get the two lifeboats on to the davits in case of sudden emergency. The other watch was set to keep throwing the coals overboard. The hose from the fire engine, which consisted of a portable force pump, was then passed down the hold and water was played on top of the coals in every conceivable place where it was thought there was fire. But through the afternoon, the smoke and gas increased to such an extent that no one was able to stop below for more than a few minutes at a time. We had got well down to the coals in the fore hatch but no actual fire could be seen. This work went on until 7pm when all of us were entirely overcome with fatigue and the effects of the gas. The Captain complimented us for working so hard to save the ship and said we had better stop for the night, but to first batten down all the hatches to smother the fire as much as possible. In case of an explosion, the fore hatch was simply put on, but not battened down, so that if there were an explosion, the decks would not blow up.

It being fine warm weather, the Captain said after we had tea we could all bring our bed mattresses to the poop and lie down there for the night, so that we would all be together, with no one forward except the man on the lookout. After tea, we considered it necessary to pack up a small bag of our clothes as no chests or anything cumbersome would be allowed in the boats. We then went aft, as directed by the Skipper, to await results. Being tired and worn out it was not long before most of us were asleep. But the sleep was not to be of long duration, for between 10 and 11 o'clock that night, heavy rumbling sounds were heard below, as if slight explosions were taking place, or that the fire and gas was making a desperate attempt to vent. No more sleep could now be had, as the noises were getting more frequent and louder. Everyone was in terror that, at any moment, the ship would blow to pieces as every explosion was making her tremble from stem to stern. Black smoke was coming from the top of the lower masts, which were built of steel, just as if they were steamboat funnels. Nothing could be done in the darkness except to await events and the approach of daylight.

Shortly after 4am, a terrible explosion was heard and all the hatches that were battened down blew off. The main hatch, which had three strong canvas tarpaulins, parted as if one had gone round the edge of them with a knife. All hands were up in an instant and the Captain went out to see what damage had been done. Clouds of jet-black smoke with an occasional flame were now coming from the hatches, the flames flickering up and down in the draught.

It was now daylight and it was plain to see that the *Teviotdale* was going fast to her doom.

Then the coat of the main mast was cut and the fire engine hose put down. The Skipper ordered the carpenter to cut a few planks out of the deck near the starboard main rigging and the hose was put down there, but it was not long before the fire came up proper at this spot where the deck was cut, and soon the decks were ablaze.

All was now confusion, but a word or two from the Captain put things right. He ordered the main and cross jack yards to be put aback to stop the ship and get the boats lowered away. Nothing had been done to the boats save putting the two lifeboats on to the davits so they were then lowered.

The longboat still lay on the chocks at the forepart of the main hatch, the best boat on the ship. The Mate said he wished to get up a coil of new rope, rig a tackle and put the longboat out by the main yard arm. However, the others thought this was not such a good idea at this critical moment, when time was precious, and one man spoke up and said, "Let us get round the boat, carry her aft and put her down using the davits." This was done in about five minutes where, if we had followed the Mate's plan, we would certainly have had to run and leave the longboat to be burned with the ship.

Provisions were placed into the boats and, as luck would have it, we had two fresh water tanks that were pumped up from the poop deck, otherwise we would have had no water since we could not, at that moment, get forward, the decks being all ablaze.

The first of the rigging to catch fire was the starboard main rigging shroud after it had fallen into the mast when the lanyards had burned. The clew garnet of the mainsail burnt and caused the clew of the mainsail to come running down with its heavy sheets and tacks. The mainsail then caught fire, setting fire one after another to the sails above till the fire reached the main royal which is the highest sail on the main mast.

We Take to the Boats

Fire aboard the Teviotdale in 1876 - Captain says "abandon ship" to the longboats.

George Jenkins dives overboard and makes it to the longboat before the sharks get him!

We were now cut off from the main deck, and had to pass the provisions up through the cabin skylight. The main mast was on the shiver as there was nothing to support it, and it was likely to break over the deck any moment. The Captain said, "Men, we had better get into the boats, I am afraid of that main mast going." I was at that time a fairly good swimmer, so I thought the easiest way to get into the boat was to take a dive from the stern and swim to her. This I did, but I had no sooner clambered into the boat when a man already in the boat drew my attention to something of a dark colour rising to the surface under the boat's quarter. He said, "My boy, you are just in time," when Mr Shark's fin came to the top of the quarter.

Sharks are very quick in the hearing and also very sharp in the eye, and are abundant in the tropical regions. He had heard the splash of me, but he was too late that time.

The Clipper Ship Teviotdale on Fire in the Indian Ocean, November 1876.

The masters and crew await their destiny as the ship is engulfed and consumed by fire.

No sooner had all hands got into the boats, and dropped astern of the *Teviotdale* with a long line fast to the ship, when the main mast with all its heavy yard attached went crashing over the side, carrying with it the mizzen top gallant mast, mizzen top mast head and the gaff. Blocks and wreckage fell on to the poop and smashed the cabin skylight rails. Had we been two minutes longer in getting into the boats, I believe half of us would have been killed by the falling wreckage.

3rd November 1876. The Teviotdale 'well ablaze' in the middle of the Indian Ocean.

With all hope of the ship lost, 'twas time to cut free the ropes, but a 100 miles from land!

7

8

Lying astern, we divided ourselves so that an equal number of men would be in each boat, there being 27 of us all told, nine being the number in each boat. The Skipper and the Mate were each in charge of the two lifeboats, and the Second Mate the longboat. As the provisions had just been thrown into the handiest boat, we shared them equally into each.

Water, we now found, would have to be dealt with very carefully and economically as we only had a small keg that held from four to five gallons for each boat; this only afforded a small glass to each man per day; not much to quench one's thirst in the tropics. The crew in each boat put a mast up, raised sails and put each boat into proper trim to make every preparation for letting go from the ship, which was now a roaring furnace from end to end, frizzling the water alongside as if she was boiling it.

All the masts were now gone, making the *Teviotdale*, which not two hours previously had been as fine and noble a ship as ever was launched from the yards of the Clyde, look like an abandoned derelict.

We kept fast to the ship until noon so that if, perchance, a passing vessel might come by, they would see the burning ship. But nothing in the shape of a vessel turned up, and at 12 o'clock we let go from what was left of the *Teviotdale* and shaped our course for the island of Diego Garcia which, by our reckoning, lay fully 100 miles away.

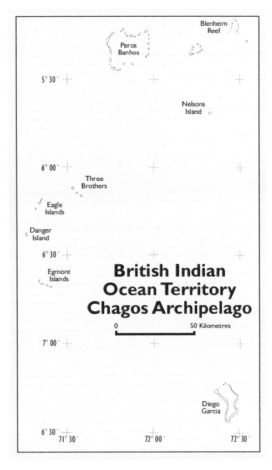

I formed one of the crew of the longboat, which we found out was the fastest of the three boats. The carpenter was also in our boat and had a few small tools with him. He converted a bucket into a binnacle to hold the compass, and it answered the purpose very well. Then, from a spare oar, he made a second mast and I provided the sail for it, utilizing one of my blankets for that purpose.

We could then sail round any of the two lifeboats, but we had to keep close to the Skipper's boat since we had to depend on him for the course to steer for the island. We were the only boat without a chronometer on board and therefore could not obtain the longitude.

Goodbye to the *Teviotdale*

Before nightfall, we had run the *Teviotdale* entirely out of sight, but the reflection of the burning ship could be seen on the horizon the whole night through. Just before darkness set in, the Captain signalled to us that he wished to speak, we then bore down on him and he said he thought it would be advisable for us that we take his painter on board our boat and make it fast to our stern for the night, in case we should get too far apart and perhaps lose one another, and this was done each following night. We then tried to get some sleep and you may guess that after all the excitement and work of trying to fight the fire, how fagged out we all were. But just fancy, with nine men in a small boat with provisions and clothes as well, the sleeping accommodation, six in a bed was nothing to it.

One man was steering our course, and the rest curled themselves up as best they could, but whenever they dropped off to sleep, they would get cramped and then, in trying to stretch their legs, some poor devil would get a foot thrust into the pit of his stomach. So you can imagine it was a night of grunts and groans and a few smothered blessings you may be sure, as each one tried to get into an easier position. I can tell you, if any one then had started to sing "Rocked in the Cradle of the Deep," he would have been promptly chucked overboard. But apart from our discomforts it was an anxious enough time. Would we manage to pick up the island all right? It was not an easy task to get a proper observation from a boat jumping about as they do with the swell of the ocean. How long would our provisions last if we should be so unfortunate as to miss it? And would we manage to reach the island without encountering any bad weather?

These were some of the questions that were speculated upon very much during our weary time in these small boats. I expect you will be able to imagine that it would certainly not have been a very comfortable "Home on the Rolling Deep". However, we escaped having any bad weather, and there was not much to relieve the monotony beyond dealing out our scanty provisions and still scantier supply of water except for an occasional sea yarn, one of which I should like to relate here to show you how little seriousness was put on the very perilous situation we were in.

It was this:

> A naval vessel had been abandoned, and the crew had taken to the boats in the same way that we had. Large Men-of-War carry nearly every sort of tradesmen and also a Minister to attend to their spiritual wants. It so happened that the Boatswain and the Boatswain's mate had got into the same boat as the Parson. Being out for several days in the boats without seeing any land, the men were beginning to become very uneasy. The Parson, hearing some of their remarks said, "How do you ever expect to see land when Bill the Boatswain has not prayed yet?"
>
> Bill spoke up and said, "Well, your Reverend, if you think it would be of any use, I will offer up a word."
>
> The Parson said, "I will be very pleased indeed Bill to hear you to do so."
>
> The next thing Bill thought of was what was he going to say and, scratching his head, he seemed to strike on something.

Down on his knees he went, and his prayer was thus: "Oh Lord God if you will send me ashore I will burn a candle as big as the mainmast."

His mate, being beside him, dug him in the ribs and whispered, loud enough for it to be heard, "Here Bill, where are you going to get a candle as big as the mainmast?"

Bill looked daggers at him, and said, "Hold your tongue you fool, when I get ashore I'll fob him off with a halfpenny one".

It was our fourth day in the boats and about eleven o'clock forenoon, the carpenter was scanning the horizon when he thought he saw the backs of some whales ahead. The sperm whale is often to be seen in those climates. The Second Mate instantly got out his binoculars, and after looking for a second gave out the welcome news, "No, it is not whales, it is the land." Still looking with his glass, he said, "That it is the island sure enough boys, let's bear down and tell the Skipper." We downed sail, put out oars and were soon alongside the Skipper's boat and gave them the news.

I can assure you, I will never forget the pleasant smiles that came on both the Skipper's face and that of the boat's crew as we gave them the glad news. The Skipper then said that as we had the swiftest boat, we had better go and tell the Mate as he was a long way astern to leeward and would not have seen the land yet. No time was put off, away we went, and it was not long before we gave them the good news also. Then we hauled our boat close to the wind to catch up with the Skipper's boat. After we had caught up with him, the wind died away and at noon it was dead calm. We downed the sails and mast and put out the oars. All three boats were now stripped of their canvas and under oars, pulling for all they were worth, and higher and higher rose the land to our view.

The sea was calm with not a breath of wind to disturb it, or cool us. The sun was scorching hot, and on and on we struggled at the oars so that we would reach the island before darkness set in. The Second Mate, who kept charge of the provisions and water, said, "Boys, I think we might indulge in an extra feed now." We had a piece of one of the cabin hams and, although it was raw with a hard biscuit, I can assure you it went down well. I thought it was the sweetest bite I had ever tasted since we were all ravenous because we had been trying to make the provisions spin out in case we missed the island.

After getting a decent drink of water each, we double-banked the oars. That is, there were two men to each oar. We pulled hard, but it was not till nine o'clock that night that we got inside the mouth of the island. The Mate was still a long way out, his crew did not seem to put on such a spurt as the Skipper's and our boat, but we were perfectly satisfied that he was all right and would lie outside the island till daybreak.

As it was now dark, the Skipper said, "We had better go no further till daylight." We were inside what looked like and proved to be a splendid and natural harbour. I understand there is a fine coaling station there now, and that some of the ill-fated Russian Fleet put in there for coal or shelter on their passage out to meet Admiral Togo during the Russian-Japanese war.

As the water was as smooth as a millpond, we made the two boats fast together, set a watch, and went to sleep very pleased to think that, from our perilous and dangerous position, we were now, so far, rescued.

At daybreak next morning, we were all anxious to see what sort of inhabitants the island contained, so we pulled towards a settlement that was nearly at the top of this natural harbour which was about eight or nine miles long. We were very pleased at nearing a little pier or jetty to see a man. It was ocular proof at least that there were no cannibals on this island with a particular relish for white men, which was something to be thankful for.

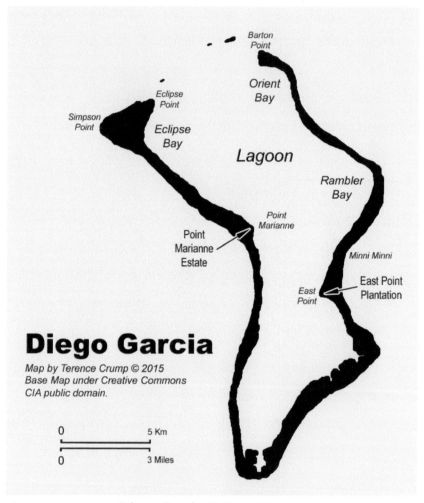

Diego Garcia © Terry Crump

This man, who was a Frenchman,[6] proved to be the only white man on the island and he was the Governor. He had about 60 workers under him

---

[6] M. Desjardins was the proprietor of Point Marianne Establishment.

engaged in collecting and extracting the oil from cocoa-nuts which grew in great abundance on the island. In fact it was the only industry there, the provisions for the Governor and workers being brought in by schooner from Mauritius every six months. This schooner also brought fresh workers out to labour, and took away those whose time had expired. It was in this schooner that our only hope lay in reaching civilization again, and we found that she had been gone about three months, so that meant we had about two and a half months to wait. However, the Governor proved himself to be a very hospitable man, provided huts for us to live in, gave us a supply of rice and also killed a pig in honour of the occasion to mark the first day of our arrival.

After getting settled down on the island, the time was spent lolling about from day to day, the only sport being bathing and fishing, and also turtle-hunting in the early morning which was very much enjoyed. In the morning, about 4 o'clock, we would get up, walk the wood of cocoa-nut trees to the west side of the island where there was, at all times, a very heavy surf rolling in on the beach of fine clean sand, then further down there was small stone, and at the edge of the surf large boulders and rocks. The turtles came through this up on to the sand and dug large holes. If not disturbed, they would lay from 120 to 140 eggs, cover them up with sand and with the strong sun striking the sand they hatched by themselves.

Shipwrecked from the Teviotdale onto a desert island in the Indian Ocean in 1876.

Surviving mainly on fish, eggs, birds, shark and turtle, the 27 survivors await rescue for 54 days.

It was when the turtle was in the sand hole that your chance lay in catching them. If you could crawl noiselessly and get on them unawares, turning them on their backs, you could then leave them with no fear of them getting on their feet again. But you had to be quick in turning them on their backs because if they mastered you and kept their feet, you had to stand clear, for in making for the water they would smother and blind you with the sand in making their escape.

Some very large turtles were caught in this way, both, by the workers and us during our stay. A very large one was caught two or three days before Christmas, killed on Christmas Eve and made a very good Christmas dinner for all of us.

The crew learn survival techniques, such as fishing for sharks off the jetty in Diego Garcia.

Though good fishing could be had, we had insufficient salt to keep our catch fresh.

Sharks were also very plentiful. I caught one about four feet long with a cod hook when fishing from the end of the little jetty, and had to draw him along the side of the jetty up on to the sandy beach in case he would break the strong line I was fishing with. Although they were plentiful, none of us seemed to be very afraid, for there was scarcely an hour of the day when some of us were not bathing.

Good fishing could be got, but the worst of it was we could not obtain sufficient salt to keep them fresh. So we gave them to the workers. However, most of us were beginning to get weary of our enforced confinement and longed for the vessel to come that brought the supplies to the island. The Governor had told us that it was a barque that always came. So when we saw a schooner beating off the island about a couple of months after landing, we thought it was a passing vessel, and the excitement amongst us was great. We launched a boat and were pulling towards her for all we were worth with our ship's ensign turned upside down on a pole as a signal of distress. We soon found that this was the vessel that was bringing the supplies for the island. However, you can imagine our disappointment when we learned that she was only going to discharge some empty casks at our island, and then had to go to another seven small islands that lay some 70 or 80 miles distant from our island to collect oil.

Rescue

So, before the schooner could come back to take us off, we just had to settle down and content ourselves for a while again. It was 21 days before she came back, but it only took two days to get everything on board from our island. Our quarters were to be down the hold, on top of the cargo, where we spread mats and old sails to make ourselves as comfortable as possible and then, as we sailed away, we waved a farewell to the Governor and our worker friends. But you may be sure we were not sorry to part, for rice and cocoa-nuts do not altogether suit a Scotch stomach and, as we had had two and half months of this, you may guess we were tired enough of it.

The Governor, however, was very good for he put a few pigs on board and a quantity of rice to help with the provisions of the schooner, as the Captain could hardly have risked taking us otherwise.

The passage to Mauritius, where the schooner was bound, occupied 13 days. When we entered Port Louis, that is the principal port for the island, none of us were permitted to go ashore that night. But next morning we were all taken to the Sailors' Home and there, the Superintendent, who also acted as Shipping Master and was the representative for the British Board of Trade, treated us very kindly.

The Superintendent was not long in spotting our cook. "Hello," he said, "surely I have seen you before." "Yes," said the cook, "I was here not so long ago with the crew of the *St. Mungo* that was also burnt out." The astonishment of the Superintendent and the way that he looked at our cook caused us to think that he regarded him as a sort of fire worshipper.

We were not long in getting settled in our new quarters and, as we were treated as distressed British Seamen, we were allowed free board and lodgings in the Sailors' Home until such time as we all obtained ships.

It was then that we all gradually became scattered, except for poor Daly who, when in the long sleeping apartment like a hospital, started in the middle of the night with a blanket round him to do his fandangos and war whoops and so thoroughly scared the other boarders, who were not used to him, that he was soon shipped and signed on at an asylum, where I afterwards heard that the poor fellow had died.

For myself, I joined a small wooden barque, belonging to Shields, called the *Hugh Bowine* and bound for Pointe de Galle in the island of Ceylon [now Sri Lanka]. From there, we got orders for Cochin and Tellicherry, two ports on the Malibar coast, there to load a general cargo for Le Havre, France.[7]

While lying at Tellicherry, the Captain and the Mate both became ill with cholera and diarrhoea and had to be sent to hospital. When all the cargo was on board, we had to wait a couple of days to give the Captain and Mate as much time as possible to recover in the hospital.

It was our usual custom when we started work in the morning to pump the ship. When we went to the pumps on the morning after the cargo had been loaded, and after pumping for fully half an hour, which was an unusually long spell, the carpenter was ordered to 'sound the pumps' and it was then discovered that the ship had sprung a leak. A survey by the different captains of the other vessels in the port was called, and their decision was that the vessel was unseaworthy and

---

[7] *Since the mid-1990s several Indian and Sri Lankan cities have reverted to local names rather the Anglicised names from colonial times. The modern place names are as follows: Pointe de Galle is now Galle, Sri Lanka; Cochin is Kochi; Tellicherry is Thalassery; and the Malibar coast is now the Malabar coast.*

would have to be dry-docked. The nearest dry dock was in Bombay, 500 miles distant along the same coast, and it was decided to take her there. For this purpose, we had to get ten local men aboard to do the pumping as the crew had enough to do to work the ship, beating her all the way, tack and tack, against the monsoons.

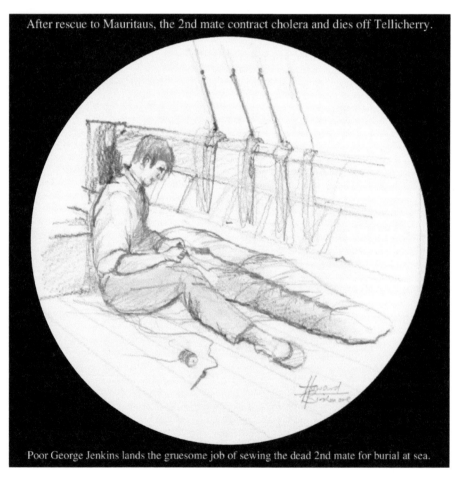

After rescue to Mauritaus, the 2nd mate contract cholera and dies off Tellicherry.

Poor George Jenkins lands the gruesome job of sewing the dead 2nd mate for burial at sea.

The Captain, so far, had recovered, but the Mate was still pretty bad. However, he insisted that he would leave the hospital and come on board, against the Captain's wishes. But the old Mate did not reach Bombay; he died three days after we left Tellicherry and was buried at sea.

The melancholy job of sowing the old fellow up in his hammock, with a bag of sand at his feet to sink the body, fell to my lot. One the saddest jobs that Jack can have to do on board a ship is to sew up one of his shipmates at sea. For, although Jack is considered a handy man, he makes a very bad undertaker.

With the help of good weather and willing men at the pumps, we all arrived safe in Bombay, the place I had originally sailed for. I had eventually got there at last; it was about the most roundabout voyage I had been on.

Homeward Bound

After all the cargo was discharged and the ship put in dry dock, I decided to leave this vessel in search of a better and bigger ship as there were, then, some fine ships lying at Bombay.

I asked the Captain to discharge me, he complied and I signed on immediately after in a large iron ship named the *Ellen Bates* of Liverpool which was bound for Liverpool.

BURNING OF THE TEVIOTDALE.

TWO MONTHS ON A DESOLATE ISLAND.

By the arrival yesterday of the master, Captain Robert Jones, at Bangor, details of the burning of the iron clipper ship Teviotdale, 1260 tons register, owned by Messrs. J. and A. Roxburgh, Glasgow, are to hand. The vessel was bound with a cargo of 1790 tons of coals, from Dundee for Bombay. She left Dundee on the 27th July last. The voyage proceeded prosperously until the 31st October, when, at five a.m. signs of fire in the cargo were discovered. The ship was then in 8 40 S. lat, and 71 40 E lon. On the following day, November 1, the hands played as much as they could with water on the coals, but were driven from the hold by the smoke and the gas. The hatches and ventilators were battened down, but at four a.m. on the 2nd they were blown up by the force of an explosion. The long boats (two) and the ship's life-boat were put over the side and provisioned. All hands, 26 in number, chiefly na-tives of Dundee, two hours afterwards took to the boats, which were dropped astern of the ship with a long line. No tidings for about six months were subsequently re-ceived of the crew, and they were supposed to be lost, until the 16th ult., when a telegram came to hand from Aden about their safety. After leaving the ship, it ap-pears the boats encountered heavy seas and drenching rain, but with several days' hard rowing they sighted Diego Garcia, and succeeded in landing there. There were two trading establishments in neighbouring islands, one at East Point and the other at Miny Miny. During their long stay of 54 days on Diego Garcia, five of the crew went over to Miny Miny, but they fell out there, and two of them returned. The manager at East Point, Mr Spurs, was very kind to the shipwrecked crew, and sent them over on different occasions sugar, sweet lemons, and vegetables, also a tubful of pickled pork, a live pig, some clean fat for their use in coking. The crew princi-pally subsisted on fish. They had been on the island about a month, when the Cape-town schooner Barso, Captain Christiensen, touched there. She left them for the Six Islands: and on December 28 she returned to Diego Garcia, and the whole of the crew of the Teviotdale embarked on board the schooner, and on the 5th January they were landed at Port Louis, Mauritius.

Extract from The British Library Board.

After 110 days' passage I arrived at that port and it was not long before I was making tracks for Bonnie Scotland again. When I landed home, I found that the voyage to Bombay and back had just occupied 15 months. I have not written of any incidents that happened on our passage home from Bombay, as I thought that this was sufficient for the time being at any rate.

If this yarn of a voyage from a sailor's point of view has given anyone here a little better idea of what Jack has to put up with at times in his rough and tumble life, or causes anyone to look a little more kindly on the poor sailors being battered and tossed about while we are lying snug in bed, then, I shall go home very well pleased to think that this yarn has not been told in vain.

George Jenkins, 1909.

The Customs House, Alloa.

Author's notes:
1   In 1909 George Jenkins was aged 53.
2   Alloa is a town in Clackmannanshire, Scotland on the banks of the Forth River.

George Jenkins with Customs House colleagues, most likely in Alloa. c1896. George, aged about 40, stands third from left.

Photo from Jenkins family archives.

Chapter Two

News of the *Teviotdale's* Voyage

It was customary during the days of sail and steam, before the telegraph became common-place, for ships' masters to record sightings and locations of every ship encountered on their journeys. This is one such sighting of the *Teviotdale* on its way round the west coast of Africa, having just passed by the Cape Verde Islands. These 'shipping news' items were then relayed back to London and then on to the ships' mother port.

Teviotdale ship sighted: spoken (sighted by...) on September 2 (1876), in latitude 8° North, longitude 23° West. This is 850 km (527 miles) off the west coast of Africa (WSW of Guinea-Bissau) and 750 km (462 miles) south of the Cape Verde Islands.

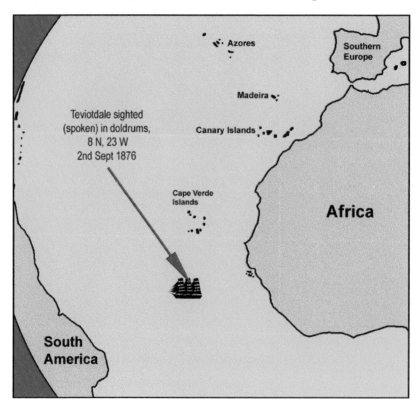

Iron clipper ship lost at sea?

Back home in Dundee, with latest news of the *Teviotdale* long overdue, the fate of the ship, her master and all her crew were probably deemed to be lost at sea. Worse news was still to come, on the 23rd of November 1876, the ship *Imperator* came alongside at a safe distance from the helpless, derelict but burning wreck of a sailing ship. All that could be determined at the time were the last four letters of her name '……dale' and her ship number 60444 on the charred remains of the bulkhead.

THE BURNING OF THE TEVIOTDALE

FIFTY-FOUR DAYS ON AN ISLAND.

Another tale of the sea, which bears a peculiar interest in this locality, is that of the burning of the Glasgow iron clipper ship Teviotdale, and her abandonment and the subsequent long sojourn of the crew on the island of Diego Garcia. The Teviotdale was owned by Messrs J. and A. Roxburgh. She was built at Glasgow in 1869. She sailed from Dundee for Bombay direct on July 27th last, laden with a cargo of 1790 tons of coals. Her crew numbered twenty-six all told, two of whom were natives of Bangor, her master, Captain Robert Jones, and the carpenter, Henry Owen, son of Mr Henry Owen, shipbuilder, Hirael. It is by the kindness of Captain Jones, who reached his residence at Llanfairpwllgwyngyll, Anglesey, by Sunday morning's mail, that we are enabled to present our readers with a full account of this shipping disaster and of the proceedings of the crew during that critical time and afterwards, they having been detained on the island mentioned for fifty-four days.

Nothing of importance transpired on the outward voyage until the 31st October. At five a.m. on that day the cook first discovered indications of the cargo being on fire. Dense smoke and noxious gas emerged from

Now with news of the burnt out wreck of the ship being encountered, those family and friends back at home; together with the ships' owners must have just about given up all hope of seeing the ship or crew of the *Teviotdale* ever again. The following article appeared in the newspaper in Bangor in March 1877.

The Final Truth of the Burning of the *Teviotdale*

Marine Board of Trade Inquiry Report

North Wales Chronicle, Saturday 10th March 1877.
Newspaper article, Page 3.

The Burning of the *Teviotdale* – Fifty-Four Days on an Island.

Another tale of the sea, which bears a peculiar interest in this locality, is that the burning of the Glasgow iron clipper ship *Teviotdale*, and her abandonment and the subsequent long sojourn of the crew on the island of Diego Garcia. The *Teviotdale* was owned by Messrs J. and A. Roxburgh. She was built at Glasgow in 1869. She sailed from Dundee for Bombay direct on July 27th last (1876) laden with a cargo of 1,790 tons of coals. Her crew numbered twenty-six all told, two of whom were natives of Bangor, her master, Captain Robert Jones, and carpenter, Henry Owen, son of Mr Henry Owen, shipbuilder, Hirael [Bangor, N. Wales]. It is by the kindness of Captain Jones, who reached his residence at Llanfairpwllgwyngyll [LLanfair PG], Anglesey, by Sunday morning's mail, that we are enabled to present to our readers with a full account of the crew during that critical time and afterwards, they having been detained on the island mentioned for fifty-four days.

Nothing of importance transpired on the outward voyage until the 31st October. At five a.m. on that day the cook first discovered indications of the cargo being on fire. Dense smoke and noxious gas emerged from the fore-hatch-way of the fore-hold. The chief officer, John Miller, who was in charge of the watch, was appraised of this, and he at once communicated with the captain. Captain Jones first tested the heat of the hold with a thermometer, and then gave directions promptly for getting the [fire] engine and rigging out the pumps. The ship was found to be on fire in 8° 40' S. latitude, and 71° 40' E, longitude. The fire engine and pumps were brought into play, and commenced to operate in the lower hold and 'tween decks, but despite the crew's strenuous efforts to get at the seat of the fire, it continued to spread. On the following day, November 1st, the hands played as much as they could with a copious stream of water on the burning coals, but were driven out from the hold at seven p.m. by the thick smoke, gas and suffocating sulphur fumes. The captain with a view, if possible, to smother the fire, ordered the hatches and ventilators to be slightly battened down; but at four o'clock on the morning of the 2nd November these were blown up with a loud explosion. The crew, however, undaunted, continued their exertions and poured volumes of water on the raging mass. But it was found that do what they would, the fire was gaining upon them, and the flames had by this fastened upon the deck. At seven a.m. the fire broke through the deck. All hopes of saving the ship were relinquished. The two long boats and ship's lifeboat were put over the side and provisioned in readiness. All hands in two hours afterwards quitted the ship and took to the boats, which were dropped astern with long towlines. At ten a.m. the main mast was burnt away about three feet below the main deck, it fell overboard with a crash and carried away with it the mizzen topmast. The foremast and mizzen mast followed and fell into the sea. The ship was now blazing furiously fore and aft, and was enveloped in smoke. The boats then finding that to stay by her was useless, shaped their course for Diego Garcia, the nearest land, and southernmost island in the Chagos Archipelago. The wind was variable at the start, with calms and heavy showers of rain. The three boats kept in company. There were nine men, under the charge of the First Office (1st Mate), Mr John Miller, in the starboard lifeboat, eight, with the Second Mate (2nd Mate), Mr George Symons in the port lifeboat, and nine and the Captain in the longboat. That day throughout they experienced a very heavy swell from the E.S.E. The next day light winds and calms prevailed accompanied by a swell in the sea. At noon, to their joy, Diego Garcia was sighted, distant about fifteen miles. On Saturday, the 4th, there was a succession of light airs and calms. Three boats pulled for the island, and at seven p.m. the longboat got round its N.W. end. In half-an-hour afterwards, the port lifeboat came up, and later the starboard lifeboat. The boats lay to all night, but at daylight proceeded up the harbour. On arriving at Point Marianne Establishment they received every kindness from the proprietor, Mr Duvergé, and the manager, Mr Desjardine. The boats were then hauled up. Next day, Sunday, some of the hands were employed fishing, and whilst the shipwrecked crew remained on the island fish was their staple food. Fishing became almost a daily occupation, and sometimes the boats were out at sea all night. On the 9th November, Captain Jones went over to East Point Establishment, and received from Mr Spurs, the manager, a large bag of sugar, and also a large basketful of sweet lemons for the crew. For the better prosecution of fishing operations, the longboat was rigged with two lug sails, staysail and jib. The weather now became hot and sultry, with occasional squalls, violent storms of thunder and lightning and heavy rains. On the 13th November, Mr Spurs sent over a basketful of sweet lemons and vegetable. A visit next day was paid by the Captain to an establishment called Miny Miny [Minni Minni], belonging to a Mr Dauvart, some distance away from Diego. On the 16th, Michael Daly, a seaman, was taken ill with fits of epilepsy. He was put in a place by himself that night, and watch kept over him. The poor man continued ill for several weeks, but at length, with careful tending, recovered. Three of the crew went over to Miny Miny on November 20th and stopped there. Mr Dauvart, the proprietor of that establishment, by the return boat sent the remainder of the crew a basketful of fish. On the 26th, three of the crew fought together, and next day the schooner *Barso*, of

Capetown, Captain Christiensen, touching at Diego, and having among her passengers a magistrate, his worship, Mr Ackroyd, landed next day, and in the presence of the whole crew censured the three quarrelsome hands for their misbehaviour. On 30th, Mr Spurs, of East Point, sent the crew a tubful of salt pork, a tubful of clean fat for cooking purposes. The lifeboat was next fitted out, like the longboat, with sails. One of the two sailors that had gone to Miny Miny came back, as he could not agree with his companion. On 4th December, Mr Spurs sent over a live pig. The 8th day was an anxious day. The lifeboat, manned by six, went out to the lower part of the harbour to fish, and did not return; the weather throughout the day was very boisterous. On the following morning, however, it moderated, and the lifeboat returned safely. Heavy gales prevailed on the 10th, and a large number of trees were torn up by the roots. On the 24th December, the schooner *Barso* came to Miny Miny Establishment, on her voyage back from Six Islands, whither she had conveyed passengers and cargo, for Port Louis, Mauritius. She had been away from the Diego group twenty-five days. Captain Jones went on board of her to arrange about having his crew taken to Mauritius. Three of the hands had by this stayed at Miny Miny for thirty-eight days. On 28th December, all shipwrecked crew, in two boats, embarked on board the schooner *Barso*, which was lying off Miny Miny, and at four p.m., the anchor was hove, and all sail set. The voyage to Port Louis was uneventful, and on the 5th January, Captain Jones and his crew landed there, having been received the best of treatment from Captain Christiensen, whose extreme kindness is officially referred to in the findings of the Marine Board of Mauritius, upon the occasion of holding an inquiry into the loss of the *Teviotdale*, and subsequent events – The ship and crew had been long ago given up as lost, no tidings having been received of the latter since 2nd Sept., when the *Teviotdale* was spoken by the ship *Imperator*. On the 23rd November she was fallen in with by a passing ship; she was then a helpless derelict, and still burning. Under the impression that she was 'missing', re-insurances were effected upon her at fifty guineas' premium. But the receipt of intelligence from Aden, on the 10th ult, of the safety of captain and crew set all anxious fears at rest. Captain Jones reached London on Friday last (2nd March), and after proceeding to Glasgow on his owner's business, returned home, as we have already stated, on Sunday morning. We regret to add that he lost all his effects when the ship had to be abandoned, but he saved the ship's log book.

Proceeding by the Board of Trade and Report

The Mauritius Marine Board assembled at the Post Office, on the 18th January, 1877, to hold an official inquiry into the burning of the ship *Teviotdale*, 1,260 tons, in lat. 8° 40' S., and long. 71° 40' E., on the 1st November, 1876, while on her voyage from Dundee to Bombay.

The members of the court were Messrs J Morgan, harbour master and president; George Davidson, Lloyd's agent; J. P. Ellis and J. Gowin, marine surveyors. – The master, Captain Robert Jones; John Miller, chief mate; George Symons, second mate; James Hawkset, sailmaker and Robert Kirkpatrick. William Keay, John Browne, and Thomas Skelly, all able-bodied seamen, members of the *Teviotdale* crew, presented themselves for examination on oath. Robert Jones, sworn, said he was 39 years of age, and Born at Bangor (Wales). I hold a masters certificate of competency No. 93,738. I commanded the *Teviotdale* since January, 1876; she was built at Glasgow in 1869 of iron. I have commanded for the last six years vessels laden with coals, trading between the United Kingdom and Bombay. The cargo was taken in at Dundee, consisting of 1,790 tons of coals. The weather was very fine in taking in cargo. When the vessel left Dundee she was tight, in good condition, well equipped and properly manned. Nothing particular occurred from the time of leaving until October 31st, when smoke was first seen issuing out of the fore-hatch; the cook gave the first alarm. The vessel was ventilated with three perpendicular Bellmouth ventilators through the main decks, two on the forecastle deck, and one on the poop, besides three up and down ventilators through the coals. I am not aware that the vessel was insured or not. There was no smell of gas or sulphur detected until the morning of the 31st October. Had such been the case the crew must have smelt it, as they had been employed for several days previous in scraping and painting the fore and after holds. I ordered the fore-hatch to be taken off, and all the articles, such as hawsers, rope & c. that were on the top of the coals to be hauled on deck. The watch was then ordered to take the coals from the main hold, and have it into the fore peak. I tried the heat in the hold through the ventilators by the thermometer, and found 76° the same as on deck; got the fire engine and force pumps ready to pump, if needed. After clearing the coals off the tween decks, I found a great deal of smoke on the starboard side about two beams before the main hatchway in the lower hold. I immediately gave orders for the fire engine to pump water on this place. The port side of the vessel, which was the lee side, seemed to be quite

THE BURNING OF THE TEVIOTDALE

PROCEEDINGS BY THE BOARD OF TRADE AND REPORT.

The Mauritius Marine Board assembled at the Post Office, on the 18th January, 1877, to hold an official inquiry into the burning of the ship "Teviotdale," 1260 tons, in lat. 8° 40' S., and long. 71° 40' E., on the 1st November, 1876, while on her voyage from Dundee to Bombay. The members of the court were Messrs J. Morgan, harbour master and president; George Davidson, Lloyd's agent; J. P. Ellis and J. Gowin, marine surveyors.—The master, Captain Robert Jones; John Miller, chief mate; George Symons, second mate; Albert Crosskey, cook; Henry Owen, carpenter; James Hawkest, sailmaker; and Robert Kirkpatrick, William Keay, John Browne, and Thomas Skelly, all able-bodied seamen, members of the "Teviotdale's" crew, presented themselves for examination on oath.

Robert Jones, sworn, said he was 39 years of age, and born at Bangor (Wales). I hold a master's certificate of competency No. 93,738. I commanded the "Teviotdale" since January, 1876; she was built at Glasgow in 1869 of iron. I have commanded for the last six years vessels laden with coals, trading between the United Kingdom and Bombay. The cargo was taken in at Dundee, consisting of 1,790 tons of coals. The weather was very fine in taking in cargo. When the vessel left Dundee she was tight, in good condition, well equipped and properly manned. Nothing particular occurred from the time of leaving until October 31st, when smoke was first seen issuing out of the forehatch; the cook gave first the alarm. The vessel was ventilated with three perpendicular Bellmouth ventilators through the main decks, two on the forecastle deck, and one on the poop, besides three up and down ventilators through the coals. I am not aware that the vessel was insured or not. There was no smell of gas or sulphur detected until the morning of the 31st October. Had such been the case the crew must have smelt it, as they had been employed for several days previous in scraping ... ng the fore and af... ... I ordered the ... ... off. ... ...uch clear of smoke and gas. The vessel's position was at noon latitude 10° 55' S., and Longitude 70° E. The weather was fine and sea smooth, all hands were turned to, some to discharge cargo from the fore-hold to the forepeak, others pumping water from both force and head pumps, and two men were sent to clear away the boats.

We continued working at the cargo, and pumping water on it until 7p.m., when the crew were driven out of the hold from the effects of the gas and smoke. I then ordered the hatches to be battened down, and all other openings to be covered and secured. At 4a.m. on the 1st November, the hatches blew off, also the covers that were over the ventilators, and a dense volume of black smoke came out of the fore-hatch-way, and up through the lower main mast head, the main mast became very much heated and the starboard waterway very hot, the fire engine was directed to play on the spot, found the fire making its way through the seams of the deck; ordered half of the crew to get the boats out, and passed them astern, whilst the remainder was trying to subdue the fire. At 7a.m. the fire broke through the decks. I then gave up all hopes of saving the ship; put the long boat in the water. The laniards [lanyards] of the main rigging on the starboard side were now on fire; ordered provisions and water to be put in the boats, and at 9a.m., all hands took to the boats, but we remained hanging onto a tow rope astern of the ship. About 10a.m. the main mast fell overboard, at about 11a.m. the fore and mizzen mast also went. The ship was now in a blaze of fire fore and aft. I then gave instructions to the boats to cast off and steer for the island of Diego Garcia. Latitude at noon 8° 20' south and 71° 48' east, and the vessel was then 97 days out from the date of leaving Dundee. I lost all my effects, with the exception of what was necessary to navigate the boats. The officers and the crew also lost their effects. Nothing further happened until we arrived at Diego Garcia on Saturday, November 4th. We were very kindly treated by Messrs Duvergé, Desjardins, Spurs, and, in fact, by every person on the island during the 54 days that we remained there. We were taken from the island and brought here by the schooner *Barso*, the master of which vessel treated us with the greatest kindness, and although his vessel was full of cargo and passengers, he did not hesitate in taking us. – The above statement being read over to the crew, they all corroborated the same.

John Miller, deposed – I am 41 years of age, born at Dundee. I hold a master's certificate of competency No. 85,193. I joined the vessel at Dundee as chief mate, before she began taking in cargo. The vessel was well ventilated. The weather was fine during the time the cargo was taken in. I am not aware from what pit the coals came. The vessel was perfectly tight, well equipped, well found, and properly manned. Nothing particular occurred up to the time the fire broke out. On the morning of the 31st October, I was in charge of the deck when the steward told me that he had been told by the cook that smoke was coming up the fore-hatch. I went down and forward to see. After watching a few minutes I observed smoke coming up from the fore-hatch; the captain came forward and ordered the hawsers and other articles to be passed on deck to get at the coals. At 6a.m. commenced turning coals from the fore-hold into the forepeak, as it was much easier to do so than to throw them overboard, with the hope of getting to the seat of the fire, if it existed. At 11a.m. the fire engine began to play on the cargo. At 11.30a.m., it became alarming, and from this time every effort was made to get at the seat of the fire and extinguish it. From this time up to 7p.m. every effort having been made on the part of the crew, they were exhausted and driven from the hold by the smoke. They rested, and the hatches were put on, the ventilators covered, and the air excluded from the hold as much as possible. At 2a.m. the hatches were opened, and we found great accumulation of smoke; we immediately closed the hatches. At 4p.m. [Author's note: should read 4a.m.] the ventilators and the hatches were blown off by an explosion with great noise, and flames issued from the main-hatch. The captain had the decks scuttled on the starboard side for the purpose of pouring water on the cargo; the rest of the crew were engaged getting the boats out, and pumping water on the cargo. Hove the ship to and lowered the boats, provisioned and dropped them astern with all hands in them; remained towing astern until 11a.m. of the 1st November. By noon all the masts had gone by the board. We finally abandoned the vessel, shaped the course for the nearest land, which was Diego Garcia, where we arrived on Saturday, the 4th November. The captain and all of us lost all our effects, the only articles we brought with us were provisions, water, and the necessary instruments for navigating the boats. During the 54 days we were at Diego Garcia, we were exceedingly well treated by the residents generally. We embarked on board the schooner *Barso*, although the vessel had more than her complement of passengers. The captain kindly took us on board and brought us here.

George Symons, deposed – I am 38 years of age, born at Dundee. I hold a Mate's certificate No. 25,262. I joined the *Teviotdale* in Dundee. The cargo was partly shipped when I joined her. The weather was very fine in taking cargo. I don't know the nature of the coals. The vessel was tight, well equipped, well found and well manned. Nothing particular happened during the passage up to the day of the fire. I was in bed; I heard people talking about fire, I arose and came on deck. On my arrival on deck, I found the watch clearing the fore-hold of hawsers, and other things that were on the top of the cargo. As soon as my watch to come on deck at 8a.m., I received orders from the captain to work the force and head pumps. I then went down in the lower hold for the purpose of ascertaining the seat of the fire. I could pass fore and aft on the port side which was the leeside of the vessel, but on the starboard, I could only get as far as the third beam from the fore-hatch on account of smoke and gas. From this time until 7p.m., all hands were employed in shifting cargo, and pumping water, doing their utmost to master the fire. At 7p.m., the crew being quite fatigued, the hatches were put on, and all other opening secured. Nothing further was done, but the usual routine until 4a.m., then the explosion took place which blew the hatches off, the covers of the ventilators, and other openings. The mast was quite hot. The captain had the decks scuttled on the starboard side, and water poured down on the cargo. About 7a.m., the fire was coming up through the openings, that had been made through the deck, the boats were got out, provisioned, watered, and manned. At 9a.m., we abandoned the vessel, but remained fast to a tow line astern, and soon after all three masts went. The boats were then cast adrift, and proceeded to the nearest land. The masts fell over the side and the vessel was in flames fore and aft.

Albert Crosskey [Author's note: Albert Cropkey according to ship's crew list], sworn, said – I am 38 years of age, born at Rye. I joined the *Teviotdale* in Dundee as cook, after the cargo was on board. We had a fine passage until fire broke out. On the morning of 31st October, at 4a.m., the fore-hatch being off, I smelt gas and saw smoke coming from the fore-hatch. I had smelt a similar smell a fortnight before, but did not report it, as I did not see smoke. I however, observed several times to the crew that I feared the ship was on fire, but had not the heart to tell the captain. I was familiar with the smell as I had experienced it on board the *St Mungo*, which vessel was from Dundee with coals, and was burnt off the Mauritius. I believe but I am not sure that both cargoes were Scotch coals. Being asked why I did not report the fire sooner, I would say that when I did report it, the mate smiled at the idea, and thought it was nonsense. In my opinion, the captain did all in his power to save the ship.

Declaration By The Remainder Of The Crew

The chief officer's evidence having been read over to us, we corroborate the above evidence, and further think that the captain did everything in his power to save the ship. On Sunday previous, the cook mentioned to some of the crew that there was a smell of gas, similar to what he had experienced on board the *St Mungo*, and he feared he was to be burnt out a second time.

We further state that we had been scraping and painting the fore and after peaks for some days previous to the fire, and there was no smell of gas to our knowledge. Henry Owen, carpenter; James Hawkset, sailmaker; William Keay, A. B.; Francis Fralen, A.B.; John Brown, A.B.; Thomas Skelly, A.B.; Robert Kirkpatrick, A.B.

The following is the official report and decision:-

The *Teviotdale* was an iron ship of 1,260 tons register, built at Glasgow in 1869, under the special survey, and owned by Messrs J. & A. Roxburgh, of Glasgow, and was commanded by Mr Robert Jones, who holds a certificate of competency as master. She left Dundee on July the 27th 1876, with a crew of twenty-six hands including the master, laden with a cargo consisting of 1,790 tons of coals, bound for Bombay direct. The *Teviotdale* was only six years and four months old, and when she left the Tay on her intended voyage was tight, staunch, well equipped and manned, and in every way a first-class ship. Nothing of importance happened from the date of her sailing until 5a.m. on the morning of the 31st October, when the cook saw and called the attention of the man on the look-out to the fact that smoke was issuing through the fore-hatch-way from the fore-hold; he also immediately reported the same to the chief mate, who was in charge of the watch. The captain was then called, who was soon at his post directing the necessary work for shifting cargo from the fore hold into the forepeak. All hands were employed during the whole day in using their best endeavours in trying to get at the seat of the fine, and pumping water on the cargo; and only ceased at 7 p.m., when driven out of the hold by the strong smell of gas and suffocating smoke. The hatches were then put on, and all the other openings leading into the hold covered over, and secured with the hope of smothering the fire. The regular watch was then set. At 4 a.m. the following morning the hatches and the covers on the different openings were blown off with a loud explosion, and a dense volume of smoke and flames issued from the hatchways, and smoke from

96

the main mast head (the lower masts were made of iron). All hands again set to work pumping water on the burning cargo through the hatchway and a scuttle which had been cut in the decks, and getting the boats out, which as soon as they were provisioned and watered were passed astern. The vessel was finally abandoned at 9 a.m., on the 1st November, but the boats remained towing astern until the whole of the masts fell overboard, and the ship was in flames fore and aft. A course was then steered for Diego Garcia, where they all arrived safely on the fore-mentioned noon of the 4th, three days after the abandonment of the vessel without incurring any further risks.

The cook in his evidence states that he thought he smelt gas for a fortnight previous to the casualty; he mentioned this to several of the men a day or two before smoke was seen issuing from the fore-hold. He also stated that the smell was similar to that which he experienced previous to being burnt out of the ship *St Mungo*, which was burnt in the Indian Ocean about three years ago, but as he did not mention this to the master or any of the officers, and as the crew had been working in the hold for several days previous scraping and painting the fore and aft peaks, and none of them was sensible of the presence of gas, it was probable that the cook's first alarm was the result of a nervous temperament.

The board are therefore of opinion that the abandonment of the *Teviotdale* was justifiable, and that the master, officers and crew only adopted this measure when all chance of saving the property entrusted to their charges had failed, and that no blame whatsoever is attached to them.

The board have now the pleasing duty of bringing to the notice of the Board of Trade the considerate and humane conduct of Captain Christensen of the schooner *Barso*, which they trust, will be recognised, who, although his vessel was deeply laden, and had in addition to her crew a full complement of passengers for this port from Diego Garcia, readily took on board his vessel this large number, twenty-six persons especially when it is borne in mind that the *Barso*, is only a small schooner of 96 tons register. Captain Christensen, who is part owner of the *Barso*, was offered payment for their transport and provisions, but he declined receiving and re-numeration. Had he refused to receive them on board, it would have entailed the chartering of a vessel specially for the purpose at a cost of at least £200.

The board also beg to notice that this is the second time within the last four months that crews of abandoned British ships have landed at Diego Garcia, and on each occasion they have been kept (hosted) for a length of time, and hospitably treated by Messrs Duvergé, Desjardins and Spurs, proprietor and mangers of the establishment. – John Morgan, Harbour Master and President of the Board; Geo. W Davidson, of Ireland, Fraser & Co., agent for Lloyd's; John P. Ellis, Marine Surveyor; John Cowin, Marine Surveyor.

Transcribed by Robert Hughes, 22nd March 2019, for Stuart Jenkins

Merchant Shipping Acts, Medals and Rewards for Rescue

The Merchant Navy has been in existence for a significant period in English and British history, owing its growth to trade and imperial expansion. The formation of Merchant Shipping Acts can be dated back to the 17th century, when an attempt was made to register all seafarers as a source of labour for the Royal Navy in times of conflict. That registration of merchant seafarers failed, and it was not successfully implemented until 1835. The merchant fleet grew over successive years to become the world's foremost merchant fleet, benefiting considerably from trade with British possessions in India and the Far East. The lucrative trades in sugar, contraband opium to China, spices, and tea, carried by ships such as the *Cutty Sark*, helped to entrench this dominance in the 19th century.

Merchant Shipping Acts

The Mercantile Marine Act of 1850 required vessels to keep official logs during the voyage which were to record illness, births, deaths, misconduct, desertions and punishments. These official logs, it should be stressed, are not logs in the usual sense of a diary or travel log, but records of masters certificates, wages, food allowances and so on. The Merchant Shipping Act of 1854 made the deposit of official logs compulsory.

Medals and Rewards for Sea Captains

It was also by the Merchant Shipping Act of 1854, the Board of Trade was given authority to award medals for acts of gallantry performed at sea. Her Majesty's Government also issues 'Rewards' to Captains who kindly took ship-wrecked sailors and passengers to a port of call whereby they could get passage back home.

Reward for the Rescue of *Teviotdale* Crew

From our research and in a response to our website relating to the fate of the *Teviotdale*, we were contacted by Bob Scarlett, a collector of Maritime Awards. Bob had in his collection a reward presented by the British Government to Captain Christensen for his rescue of the crew of the *Teviotdale*.

1878 .				REWARDS GIVEN BY HER
Rotation No.	Registered No.	Name and Ship of Recipient.	Nationality.	Particulars of Service.
138	2423	Capt. Christensen of the Schooner "Barso" of Copenhagen	Dane	For his kindness & humanity in conveying the Master & 25 of the crew of the "Teviotdale" of Glasgow which was burnt in the Indian Ocean on 1st November 1876 from the Island of Diego Garcia which they had reached in their boats, to the Mauritius where they were landed on 11th Jany 1877

From the records that Bob Scarlett provided us with, we have proof that the master and part-owner of the schooner *Barso*, a

Captain Christensen, came to the rescue of our ship-wrecked sailors and was awarded a gift for his kindness and humanity in providing passage from the island Diego Garcia to Port Louis in Mauritius.

1878				REWARDS GIVEN BY HER MAJESTY'S GOVERNMENT							1878
								Dates			
Award Number	Register Number	Name and Ship of Recipient	Nationality	Particulars of Service	Name and Port of Ship to which Services were rendered	Subsistence Money, and whether claimed or not.	Nature and Value of Reward	When Ordered	When Received	When Presented	Remarks
138	2423	Capt. Christensen of the Schooner "Barso" of Copenhagen	Dane	For his kindness humanity in conveying the Master and 25 of the crew of the 'Teviotdale' of Glasgow which was burnt in the Indian Ocean on 1st November 1876 from the Island of Diego Garcia, which they had reached in their boats, to the Mauritius where they were landed on 11th January 1877.	Teviotdale' Sch. (Schooner) Glasgow	The 'Barso' was put to little or no inconvenience with regards to the subsistence of the crew.	Binocular £10	H 27.2	18.3.78	F.O. Rec'd 4397	----

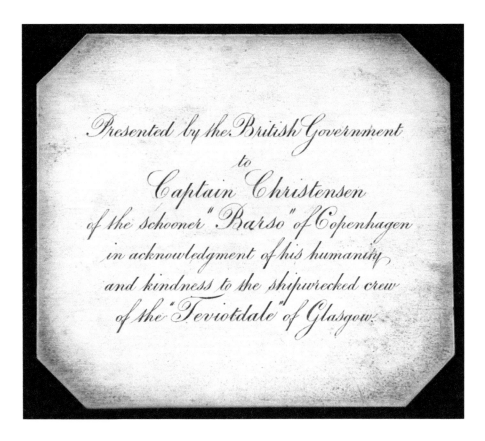

The wording on the beautiful dark wood presentation case belonging to the binoculars, reads as follows:

Presented by the British Government

to

Captain Christensen
Of the schooner "Barso" of Copenhagen
In acknowledgement of his humanity
and kindness to the shipwrecked crew
of the "Teviotdale" of Glasgow.

The gifts for rewards were procured by the Board of Trade from a selection of high quality sources, these binoculars were made by Troughton and Simms, one of the finest instrument makers in the country. As can be seen in the extract below from Her Majesty's Government register of rewards, a variety of other gifts were presented as rewards, items such as: Silver Dessert Dish £18.6s.0d (#136), Gold Watch £25 (#137), Binoculars £10.0s.0d (#138) and Silver Guilt Tankard £21.1s.0d. (#139).

1878.	REWARDS GIVEN BY HER MAJESTY'S GOVERNMENT.						1878.

Another newspaper, *The Otago Witness*, from New Zealand, reports of the *Teviotdale* burned out as follows:

'The ship *Breadlebane*, from San Fransico, arrived at Queenstown, March 5th. Reported having passed, December 2nd, an iron vessel of about 1,400 tons, burned to the water's edge. DALE, part of her name, was visible. Mitchell's Register of March 9th. Says:- "Captain Robert Jones, late Master of the iron ship *Teviotdale*, of Glasgow, arrived Bangor on Tuesday, bringing full particulars of the destruction of that vessel in 8deg. 40min. S. latitude, and 70deg. E longitude."'

The newspaper report goes on to detail much of what we know about the fire and ensuing shipwreck of the sailors, along with their sojourn on Diego Garcia and their rescue to Mauritius.

103

English Shipping.

The ship Breadalbane, from San Francisco, arrived at Queenstown, March 5th. reported having passed, December 2nd, an iron vessel of about 1400 tons, burned to the water's edge. DALE, part of her name, was visible

Mitchell's Register of March 9th, says:—"Captain Robert Jones, late Master of the iron ship Teviotdale, of Glasgow, arrived at Bangor on Tuesday, bringing full particulars of the destruction of that vessel, in 8deg. 40min. S. latitude, and 70deg. E longitude. The Teviotdale was owned by Messrs J. and A. Roxburgh, of Glasgow, and sailed on July 27th last, laden with a cargo of 1790 tons of coal, from Dundee for Bombay direct. She had a crew of 26 hands, principally belonging to Dundee and Aberdeen. Nothing of importance occurred until October 31st, at 5 a.m., when the cook observed smoke issuing from the forehold. This was reported to the chief mate, John Miller, and next to the captain, who at once gave directions about shifting the cargo; n l getting the fire engine and pumps to play in the lower hold and 'tween decks. All day the crew did their best to get at the seat of the fire, and on the following day these exertions were resumed, but they were driven from the hold by the smoke, sulphur, and gas The hatches and ventilators were then battened down with the view of smothering the fire, but at 4 a.m. on November 2, they were blown up by a violent explosion. The crew continued to play upon the burning mass, but it was ound that the deck had ignited, and at 7 a.m the flames broke through. The masts, one by one, fell overboard : all hopes of saving the ship were then abandoned, and the two longboats and ship's lifeboats were launched and provisioned. The ship being nothing but one huge blaze both fore and aft, the boats left and steered for Diego Garcia, the southernmost island of the Chagos Archipelago, which, after several days and nights' hard rowing and exposure to heavy seas and bad weather, they succeeded in making. Upon this island they remained for 54 days, subsisting principally upon what fish they could catch. One man was prostrated by epilepsy, but recovered. On the 28th December the shipwrecked crew were taken off by the Cape Town schooner Barso, Captain Christianson which had touched there on her way from Port Louis, Mauritius, to Six Islands. On the 5th January they were landed at Port Louis."

Later still, reports were coming in of a large derelict hulk traversing the Indian Ocean, causing a danger to shipping in this sea. This was of course, the charred remains of *Teviotdale*. News came from a ship two days out of Aden called the *Hindostan*. The report was posted on 17th September 1877, nearly a year after the ship had set sail from Dundee.

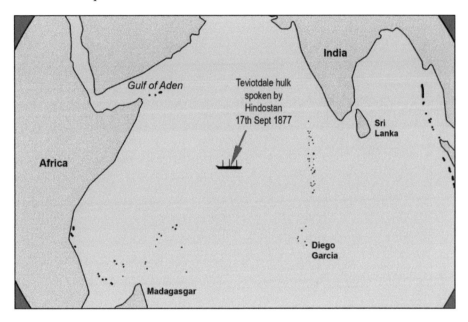

Title: The *Hindostan* sights a smouldering hulk in the Indian Ocean, 1877. Map: Robert Hughes.

Report reads:

17/9/1877 P&O steamer HINDOSTAN encountered smouldering hulk of TEVIOTDALE two days out from Aden, in 1°48'N 62°36E. The Mauritius Marine Board considered the abandonment was justified.

Hindostan, #47634, Iron Sailing Vessel, 3 Masted Ship. 833 tons, 182.4ft length, built 1863, launched 12th Nov 1863, John Reid, Port Glasgow. Passenger/cargo. *Hindostan* renamed *Waitara* in 1874 by new owners: New Zealand Shipping Co.

Chapter Three

Previous Missions and News of the Teviotdale.

1873   It was customary for shipping companies to publish future planned sailings in the local and regional newspapers such as *The Aberdeen Journal and General Advertisers*. Today, these sources provide fascinating insights into voyages of the past, since it is in this newspaper that we find an advertisement for a planned voyage to Melbourne, Australia in the January of 1873.

NOTICE TO INTENDING PASSENGERS TO MELBOURNE.

Glasgow Shipping Company's Line of Clipper Packets.

"Teviotdale Iron Ship, 1,260 Tons Reg'd."
Captain Nicol, To sail clipper packet ship to and from Melbourne, Australia on14th February 1873.

The attention of intending passengers is requested to the Magnificent Vessels of this Line, built by eminent Clyde Shipbuilders specially for the trade, fitted out with every modern improvement and convenience. They combine great strength with speed and are commanded by experinced Officers. The passages they have made have been the quickest of any Line out of Great Britain.

The following Packet will sail punctually from Glasgow on the date advertised:-
Ship. TEVIOTDALE, Iron Ship, Tons Reg'd. 1,260, Captain. Nicol, To sail. 14th February (1873).

Parties at Home, or in the Colonies, can make arrangements with the Company's Agents for the Passages of Friends either to or from Melbourne.

PASSAGE MONEY-
    CABIN.........................£40 Sterling
    INTERMEDIATE.........£18 Sterling
    STEERAGE................£16 Sterling
For further particulars, apply to
    AITKEN, LILBURN, & CO., Managers,
        86, Buchanan Street, Glasgow,
or to JOHN COOK, Esq., 48, Marischad Street, Aberdeen.

1873   The *Teviotdale* did indeed succeed in sailing to Melbourne; it is recorded to have left a few days later than planned, which can be seen from the Shipping News as reported in the *Dundee Courier* of Saturday 22nd February 1873. The newspaper records the departure as being on 20th February with Captain Nicol in charge as he departed Glasgow. See article below of which the relevant entry transcribes as follows:

Shipping News – Maritime Extracts

Teviotdale Nicoll, left Greenock for Melbourne, 20th inst. (20 Feb 1873)

SHIPPING NEWS.

ARRIVALS AT DUNDEE.
CAMPERDOWN DOCK.
February 20. –Anglia (s.), Speedie, London, goods ; Pladda (s.), Gloak, Tyne, goods.
EARL GREY'S DOCK.
February 21.—Curfew (s.), M'Kechnie, Sunderland, coals.

MARITIME EXTRACTS.
Ellon Castle, Lyall, at Shanghae from Keelung, 3d ult.
Lammermuir, left   do.   for Hong Kong, 2d ult.
Jean Stewart, off Cape Otway for Sydney, 1st ult.
Wressel Castle, left Newcastle, N.S.W., for Manila, Dec. 10.
Ellen Kerr, left Dieppe for London, 18th inst.
Invermark, M'Kenzie, at Elsinore for Stettin, 19th inst.
Tornado, at Pensacola from Clyde, 27th ult.
Chippewa,   do.   do., 30th ult.
Teviotdale, Nicoll, left Greenock for Melbourne, 20th inst.
Marian Moore, at Galle from Diamond Harbour, 27th ult.
Bengal, at Batavia from Cheribou, 8th ult.
County of Stirling, left Batavia for Siam, 9th ult.
Montrose,   do.   Channel, 16th ult.
Her Majesty, at Hong Kong from Foochoofoo, 14th ult.

Dundee Courier - Saturday 22 February 1873

Author's note (for abbreviations used in newspaper articles of the time):

1. inst. (instant) = present or current month.
2. ult. (Ultimo Mense, Latin) = last month.

1875 July During our research on the sailing missions of the *Teviotdale*, we found a report of a life lost at sea. See location map on page 113.

```
Ship "Teviotdale"
AJHR 1876 Section H26 page 13
Return of Wrecks

Date of Casualty        : 29 Jul 1875
Name of Master          : Lauchlan NICOL
Age of Vessel           : 6 years, Aa1 100 Lloyd's
Rig                     : Ship
Register Tonnage        : 1259
Number of Crew          : 26
Number of Passengers    : 31
Nature of Cargo         : General
Nature of Casualty      : Loss of life
Number of Lives Lost    : 1
Place of Accident       : Lat. 42o 39'S., Long. 62o 12'E
Wind Direction          : SSE
Wind Force              :


Finding of Court of Inquiry
Nil.
```

Credit to http://archive.is/nOMLp.

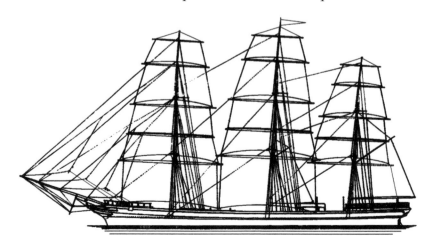

A transcription of the digital record of the report is as follows:

```
Ship  "Teviotdale"
AJHR 1876 Section H26 page 12
Return of Wrecks

Date of Casualty:      29 Jul 1875
Name of Master:        Lauchlan Nicol
Age of Vessel:         6 years, Aa1 100 Lloyd's
Rig:                   Ship
Register Tonnage:      1259
Number of Crew:        26
Number of Passengers:  31
Nature of Cargo:       General
Nature of Casualty:    Loss of Life
Number of Lives Lost:  1
Place of Accident:        Lat. 42o 39's., Long. 62o 12'E
Wind Direction:        SSE
Wind Force:
```

Finding of Court of Inquiry
Nil.

1875 August   There is documented evidence that the *Teviotdale*, under the command of Captain Nicol voyaged to New Zealand, calling in to Wellington on 26th August 1875. Below is our reference to the list found in the New Zealand Migrant Shipping Register 1861-1875 (*White Wings*, Henry Brett). See ref ① in figure below.

Vessel	Day	Mth	Year	Arrived	Tons	Captain
Teviotdale	26	08	1875	Wellington	1,260	Nicol

New Zealand Migrant Shipping (1861-1875)

The following index was based on a list which the Computing Group at the New Zealand Society of Genealogists placed in the public domain in 1988. The index lists the ships mentioned in Sir Henry Brett's two volumes of *White Wings*, which were published in Auckland in 1924 and 1928 respectively.

Arrivals of local and overseas voyages were recorded at Auckland, Bluff, Dunedin, Napier, Nelson, New Plymouth, Otago, Port Nicholson, Timaru, Wanganui and Wellington. Page numbers for further information are indicated in the 'SRC' column.

VESSEL	DAY MTH YEAR	ARRIVED	DAY MTH YEAR	DEPARTED	PASS	TONS	DAYS	CAPTAIN	SRC	COMMENTS
FERNGLEN	29 04 1875	Auckland	.. ..	... ...	...	800	...	Fraser	230	... ...
TINTERN ABBEY	03 05 1875	Lyttelton	07 01 1875	England	309	1556	...	P.B.Stevens	162	18 deaths en route.
TIMARU	06 05 1875	Port Chalmers	05 01 1875	England	...	1300	121	Rankin	160	... ...
CICERO	18 05 1875	Lyttelton	.. ..	... ...	...	1130	...	Raymond	230	... ...
DUNEDIN	18 05 1875	Lyttelton	13 02 1875	England	...	1250	94	Whitson	145	... ...
CITY OF CASHMERE	21 05 1875	Port Chalmers	.. ..	... ...	...	1000	...	Torrance	230	... ...
HINDOSTAN ②	22 05 1875	Wellington	10 02 1875	London (Information provided by Denise & Peter Wells of Wellington, NZ)						
EARL OF ZETLAND	03 06 1875	Port Chalmers	.. ..	... ...	...	1461	...	Reid	231	... ...
COUNTESS OF KINTOR	08 06 1875	Napier	18 03 1875	England	...	700	82	Braddick	61	... ...
HANNIBAL	09 06 1875	Wellington	.. ..	... ...	...	1191	...	Brown	231	... ...
JOHN NORMAN	11 06 1875	Napier	.. ..	... ...	...	...	...	...	231	... ...
DUNMORE	30 06 1875	Nelson	.. ..	... ...	...	500	...	Hastings	231	... ...
LANARKSHIRE	08 07 1875	Lyttelton	.. ..	... ...	...	796	...	Swinton	231	... ...
COLLINGWOOD	10 07 1875	Wellington	18 04 1875	London	...	1-14	...	Black	231	

VESSEL	DAY MTH YEAR	ARRIVED	DAY MTH YEAR	DEPARTED	PASS	TONS	DAYS	CAPTAIN	SRC	COMMENTS
ROBINA DUNLOP	21 07 1875	Auckland	.. ..	... ...	...	493	...	Jack	231	... ...
WHITE ROSE	21 07 1875	Lyttelton	14 02 1875	London	166	1556	137	Thorpe T.G.	161	... ...
ORIANA	24 07 1875	Lyttelton	.. ..	... ...	...	997	...	Guthrie	231	... ...
ALDERGROVE	25 07 1875	Port Chalmers	30 04 1875	Greenock	...	1270	...	Fullerton	231	... ...
LUTTERWORTH	26 07 1875	Auckland	13 04 1875	England	...	883	103	Pearson	133	... ...
WOODLARK	03 08 1875	Otago	02 05 1875	London	...	867	85	Largie	134	... ...
JAMES NICOL FLEMING	04 08 1875	Port Chalmers	06 05 1875	London	280	1000	90	Gale	69	... ...
ALUMBAGH	17 08 1875	Auckland	.. ..	... ...	...	1138	...	Lowe	231	... ...
BLAIRGOWRIE	24 08 1875	Lyttelton	.. ..	... ...	...	1550	...	Darke	231	... ...
TEVIOTDALE ①	26 08 1875	Wellington	.. ..	... ...	...	1260	...	Nicol	231	... ...
JOHN RENNIE	27 08 1875	Auckland	.. ..	... ...	...	874	...	Nicholson	231	... ...
RODNEY	29 08 1875	Wellington	.. ..	... ...	...	1447	...	Louttit	231	... ...
ALTCAR	30 08 1875	Port Chalmers	.. ..	... ...	...	1283	...	Harvey	231	... ...
HALCIONE	02 09 1875	New Plymouth	.. ..	... ...	...	842	...	Croker	231	... ...

Credited source:
http://members.iinet.net.au/~perthdps/shipping/mig-nz2.htm

1876 The *Teviotdale* was seen 'scudding' along up the English Channel on her way home through this narrow and busy strait of water. Observed officially by the Dover Coastguard, the information duly telegraphed onwards to Lloyds of London. She would have docked some 12 hours later in Dundee, Scotland.

It was the finding of this news report that led to the commission, by Stuart Jenkins, for the painting of the *Teviotdale* to be created. This first painting in the series, called 'Scudding', celebrates the life and achievements of the *Teviotdale*, George Jenkins and his family and commemorates the safe return of the ship on its penultimate journey.

1877 5th May   *Breadalbane* reported 'burned out hulk', news article from a New Zealand Newspaper.

1877 17th September, shipping news.

It is interesting to note that the Peninsular and Orient (P&O) steamer *Hindostan* (see ref ②), which called in to Wellington on 22nd May 1875 is the same ship that reported an encounter of a smouldering hulk (the *Teviotdale*) on 17th September 1877, two days out from Aden in 1°48'N 62°36E. In fact, the smouldering hulk had been a shipping hazard, circulating in the currents and winds of the Indian Ocean for nearly 10 months. See extract of evidence below.

A VESSEL ON FIRE FOR TEN MONTHS.—Information received from Lloyd's states that the Peninsular and Oriental mail steamer Hindostan, arrived at Suez from China, reports that "on the night of the 17th of September, two days before reaching Aden, she boarded a vessel which had apparently been abandoned on fire, probably some weeks previously. She was completely gutted, but the coal was still smouldering in her hold. She was identified as the Teviotdale of Glasgow, by the official number and registered tonnage marked on the main-hatch beam. The iron ship Teviotdale, bound from Cardiff [*Dundee] to India, with a cargo of coals, was abandoned on fire on the 1st November, 1876, in lat. 11 south, long. 70 east, near the Mauritius, and has thus drifted about 2000 miles in ten months. The crew were picked up soon after abandoning the vessel [** The crew were rescued to Mauritius some 60 days later].

Source: http://archive.thetablet.co.uk/article/13th-october-1877

*, ** Editor's corrections. 2019.

For more details and photograph of *Hindostan*, see www.clydeships.co.uk.

Chapter Four

The Chagos Archipelago and Diego Garcia

Diego Garcia is in the Chagos Archipelago south of the Equator in the Indian Ocean, 1,825 km (1,134miles) SSW of India, roughly halfway between Madagascar (off the east coast of Africa) and Sumatra, Indonesia.

Diego Garcia is the largest of about 60 islands in the Archipelago. There are five main groups of islands. Diego Garcia is an atoll and its rim stretches for a total length of about 64 km (40miles).

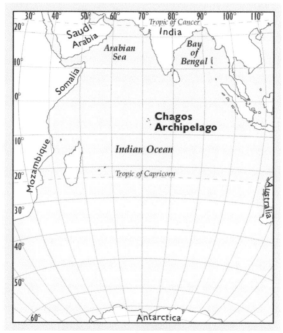

Map credit: Terence Crump.

The extent of this atoll covers about 170 km^2 (66 square miles), the lagoon is about 120 km^2 (46 square miles) and around 30 km^2 (12 square miles) is land mass. The land mass is in a 'U' shape, the opening at the top contains three smaller islands.

Today, Diego Garcia is part of the British Indian Ocean Territory (BIOT), an overseas territory of the United Kingdom, formed when the Chagos Islands were detached from the British Colony of Mauritius in 1965.

Diego Garcia and the other 60 smaller islands in the Chagos Archipelago were totally uninhabited places until the late 18th century and therefore do not have any indigenous people. These uninhabited islands are asserted to have been discovered by the Portuguese navigator, explorer, and diplomat Pedro Mascarenhas in 1512, first named as Dom Garcia, in honour of his patron, Dom Garcia de Noronha when he was detached from the Portuguese India Armadas during his voyage of 1512–1513. However, the French visited from Mauritius in 1778 and collected coconuts and fish. Records show 'a dozen huts' occupied by Frenchmen around 1786 when the British East India Company tried to settle there in April 1786. Records show there were about 275 settlers at the time, who were overwhelmed by 250 survivors of the shipwreck of a British East India ship *Atlas* in May. By October, the colony had failed. After the British had left, the French began marooning lepers on Diego Garcia, and in 1793 the French began a coconut plantation based on imported workers. Exports from the plantation were coconut fibre, sea cucumbers and coconuts.

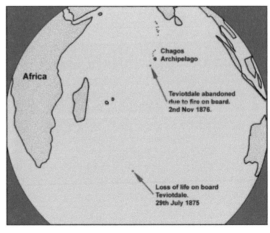

Map credit: Robert Hughes

After the Napoleonic Wars (1769-1821), Diego Garcia was handed to the United Kingdom as part of the 1814 Treaty of Paris and was administered from Mauritius. East Point on the eastern rim was the former main settlement during the time when the plantations of coconuts and copra were in operation. Minni Minni, north of East Point and Pointe Marianne on the western rim were also areas of settlement involved in the extraction of the copra and oil from the coconuts. All the settlements were located on the inlet (lagoon) side of the atoll rim. The majority of the workers lived at these locations, though there were several villages scattered around the island.

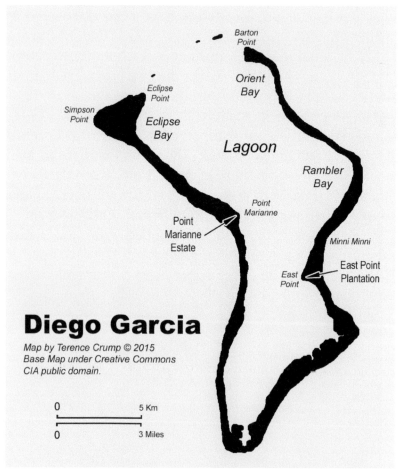

Map credit: © 2015 Terence Crump.

During the second half of the nineteenth century, when the British Empire established a global network of coaling stations to supply its fleet, Diego Garcia briefly based two coaling stations for the Royal Navy's steamships crossing the Indian Ocean. In the 1880s

114

the island witnessed an increasing movement of trading and warships, symbols of Britain's imperial century. The coaling stations were in operation from 1881 until 1888.

This is from *Trove* newspaper archives:

DIEGO GARCIA COALING STATION. TO THE EDITOR OF THE HERALD.

Sir,—As agents for Mr. William Lund (who has formed a coaling station, with a stock of 4,000 tons coal, at Diego Garcia), we enclose a copy of his letter which appeared in Mitchell's Maritime Register, giving particulars in reference to the island and the facilities for coaling steamers.

We are, &c. Sydney, January 4. GILCHRIST, WATT, and CO. Diego Garcia.

18, Jewry-street, Aldgate, London, E. C., Oct. 28, 1882.

Dear Sir,—I notice in Lloyd's List of yesterday a description of this island, and, for the information of your committee and members, I wish to give you a few more details. In January, 1881, the steamer *Delcomyn*, on her voyage from London to Australia, visited this island, and found the harbour all that is now described by the Orient Steam Navigation Company. In July, 1881, I despatched the barque *Eleanor*, with coals, from London direct to the island, where she arrived on October 30, and there and then established the first coaling depot on that island, under the superintendence of Mr. George Worsell, who has been in my employ since 1874.

H. M. S. *Ready* was supplied with the first coal by me at Diego Garcia on October 31, 1881, and was the first ship that ever coaled there. On January 17, 1882, I further despatched the barque *Talavera*, also from London with coals, arriving there on May 10, and both these vessels are now stationed at East Point as store ships, and connected with the shore by a landing stage. Since then the *Norham Castle* and *Mary Fry* have arrived out, on

June 6 and September 29 respectively, and with the ship *Superb*, from Cardiff (on August 26), on the way, I shall have a stock of about 4,000 tons coal to supply my own, as well as other boats, in the Australian trade. Like Eastern and Middle Islands, held by the Orient Steam Navigation Company, so has Western Island, which commands the entrance to the harbour, been leased to me by the Mauritius Government for 50 years, and as the deep water channel enters close by this island, I have erected a flagstaff on it for the guidance of shipmasters. Although the surf rolls very heavily at times, there is no danger whatever in entering the harbour, after which Mr. Worrell has placed buoys, at intervals, as far as East Point; and on entering, steamers should keep these buoys on the starboard side all the way. The distance from West Island to East Point is from seven to eight miles, and in proof of the easy progress up the harbour, I would mention that the sailing ship *Norham Castle* beat against a south-east monsoon in 11 tacks from West Island to East Point. 'Ballast' is plentiful, and easily worked by iron lighters, and good fresh water and fish are abundant. The climate is healthy, and hurricanes are not known. The following steamers have coaled at East Point coaling depot:—*Delcomyn* (five times), *Yeoman*, *Sorrento*, *Wodan*, *Catania*, and H. M. S. *Ready*; and the following steamers have received coaling orders:—*Gulf of Carpentaria*, *Europa*, *Glendower*, *Glen Ochill*, *Explorer*, *Sikh*, *Afghan*, *Gulf of Suez*, and *Essex*. At all times willing to give you any further information, I remain, dear sir, yours truly, W. Lund. The secretary Lloyd's.

Historically, its strategic geographic location in the Indian Ocean, south of India and halfway between Africa and Indonesia, enabled tiny Diego Garcia to play a significant role for Britain's interests in the area and beyond.

Coconut plantation (palm oil)

During the 1860s Diego Garcia was a major producer of copra (coconut oil). Minni Minni was in the area of a large plantation and the location of an operation for the processing of coconuts, copra and coconut oil.

Coconut oil, or copra oil, is an edible oil extracted from the flesh of mature coconuts harvested from the coconut palm. It has various applications. Because of its high saturated fat content, it is slow to oxidize and more resistant to rancidification, copra oil can last up to six months at 24°C (75°F) without spoiling. Proper harvesting of the coconut (the age of a coconut can be 2 to 20 months when picked) makes a significant difference in the efficacy of the oil-making process. Copra made from immature nuts is more difficult to work with and produces an inferior product with lower yields.

Dry processing requires that the flesh be extracted from the shell and dried using heat such as fire, sunlight, or kilns to create copra. The copra is pressed or dissolved with solvents, producing the coconut oil and a high-protein, high-fibre mash. The mash is of poor quality for human consumption and is instead fed to ruminants; there is no process to extract protein from the mash. A traditional way of making coconut oil utilised a powered mill driven by a domesticated animal such as a donkey or ox.

References:

Wikipedia (https://en.wikipedia.org/wiki/Diego_Garcia#History)

Research has brought to light a document by D. R. Stoddart who wrote about the settlement and development of Diego Garcia in 1971.

The document quotes the output of copra oil from the islands as being in the region of 450,000 litres per annum.

prohibition. In 1864, the output at Diego Garcia was as follows:

East Point	34 000 veltes	(51 000 gallons)	232 000 litres
Marianne	20 000 veltes	(30 000 gallons)	136 000 litres
Minni Minni	12 000 veltes	(18 000 gallons)	82 000 litres
Total	66 000 veltes	(99 000 gallons)	450 000 litres

These figures seem extremely high: at about 24 lbs of copra per velte of oil, representing about 75 nuts, it indicates a total yield of nearly five million nuts. Assuming 800 nuts to the acre, i.e. not particularly intensive or well-managed plantations, this would indicate that almost the whole area of the atoll (6250 out of 7488 acres) was being cropped for coconuts. These rough calculations simply indicate the order of magnitude of the operations at this time. Under the new administrative arrangements, the government retained the right to resume up to two acres in each property for any government purpose. The powers of magistrates for the island dependencies were defined in 1872, and in 1875 the first regular magistrate's tour was made by E. P. Brooks (Brooks 1876). The total Diego Garcia oil production of 66 000 veltes in 1864 compared with 13 500 on Salomon, 26 000 on Peros Banhos, 11 870 on Egmont, and 8 000 on Eagle (Lane 1956b, 671-3).

The three estates on Diego Garcia were amalgamated in 1883 under the Société Huilière de Diégo et Péros. James Spurs, the company manager at East Point, who later went to Aldabra, was a remarkably capable and enlightened man. He had strict regulations over liquor consumption, and ran his plantations in a benevolent if despotic manner. His labourers were expected to collect, dehusk and break 500 nuts a day, and the women to scoop out 1200 shells a day. There were hospital buildings on each of the estates.

The two coaling stations are mentioned as being located at East Point and Minni Minni under the control of James Spurs (Orient Company) and G. Worrel (Lund Company) respectively. The coals being held in ship hulks anchored off both East Pont and Minni Minni.

The three estates on Diego Garcia were amalgamated in 1883 under the Société Huilière de Diégo et Péros. James Spurs, the company manager at East Point, who later went to Aldabra, was a remarkably capable and enlightened man. He had strict regulations over liquor consumption, and ran his plantations in a benevolent if despotic manner. His labourers were expected to collect, dehusk and break 500 nuts a day, and the women to scoop out 1200 shells a day. There were hospital buildings on each of the estates.

D. The Coaling Stations

In 1881 the Orient Steam Navigation Company gave up its coaling station at Aden and surveyed Diego Garcia as an alternative. The Company operated twelve ships on the England to Australia run, and in 1882 it opened the first coaling station on Diego Garcia. The London company of G. Lund opened a second coaling station in the same year: it had only two cargo ships plying between England and Australia, but proposed to sell coal to any ship which called. Both Orient and Lund began at East Point. Orient employed James Spurs, who had resigned as manager for the Société Huilière, as their agent on the atoll, and imported both Somali and European labour. Lund appointed G. Worrell as local agent, and used local labour when required. The coal stocks were kept in hulks anchored off East Point and Minni Minni, and Orient also had yards on shore at East Point. At the time of the Magistrate's visit in 1883 there was a stock of 15,000 tons of coal at the atoll, two-thirds of it belonging to Orient. The target of the operators was to fuel 180 ships a year, each turning around in 24-68 hours; passengers were not allowed to go ashore.

43. The Manager's house and other buildings at East Point: The railway leads to the jetty

44. Copra-drying sheds and the church at East Point

The Chagos Archipelago's Future?

After many years of conservation, in an attempt to remove many
species of 'human' introduced flora and fauna, most of the
islands are being returned to nature. Finally, in 2010, the Chagos

Marine Protected Area (MPA) was declared to cover the waters around the Chagos Archipelago. However, Mauritius objected to the MPA and since this date there has been conflict between the two parties. Although the conflict still continues, much work has been done in the conservation of the archipelago.

Refer to Chagos Conservation Trust: https://chagos-trust.org/

Witness to Neptune's Moods

The visiting magistrates did not just reveal conditions on land; their adventures at sea exposed, for the first time, what the islanders had long experienced in their passages to and from Mauritius. The seasonal variations in weather, described in Chapter 1, could be a matter of life and death. During the 1870s alone, one supply ship, the *Adeline*, was in 1874 simply lost at sea. In 1879, Dupont himself 'was wrecked at Agalega while aboard a French barque, the *Myosotis*. He did not get away until four months had elapsed'. Less than a year later, 'the French vessel *Africa* was wrecked on Eagle Island ... She was taking labourers there & supplies, the anchorage at this place being for sailing vessels almost as bad as that of Agalega'.

More often the voyages entailed infinite varieties of endurance, as often through calm as storm. This was true even for short distances within the Archipelago. For example, in 1876, the schooner *Barso* took 11 days to sail the 70 miles separating Diego Garcia from Six Islands. In November the following year, this time aboard a much bigger vessel, 'the passage was a very trying one, as the *Virginie*, though a good vessel in some respects, was ill adapted for a tropical voyage' – and this time it took 47 days to reach Eagle Island. There, variable winds made things difficult enough, but on reaching Salomon (on 7 January 1878), there was too little wind for the *Virginie* to enter the lagoon; next day Ackroyd was rowed in over the reef in a boat sent out to collect urgently needed supplies. The brig followed on 10 January. After a failed attempt to depart on 17 January, she got clear of the lagoon a day later, but succeeded only in drifting into the Peros Banhos lagoon, which she was unable to leave until the 22nd.

Between June and September, high winds and heavy seas were the norm. For example, in July–August 1877, the barque *Eva Joshua* (285 tons) took 28 days to reach Diego Garcia, 'occasioned by strong head winds and heavy seas, which compelled the captain to keep

Diego Garcia and The *Teviotdale*

Shortly after creating the website telling the story of the fate of the *Teviotdale*, we were contacted by Mr Nigel Wenban-Smith, a retired diplomat and chairman of Friends of the Chagos (now the Chagos Conservation Trust).

Nigel wrote to Stuart with this information:

First, here is the part of the report, from which I first learned about the loss of the *Teviotdale*. It comes from the report of one of the first Visiting Magistrates to the Chagos Islands, John Ackroyd. It is in a file in the National Archives at Kew, number CO 167/573.

The main paragraph mentioning the *Teviotdale* read as follows:

'102. Though not strictly within the scope of my report, I trust I may be permitted to mention the generous and human conduct of Mr. Desjardins, Manager of Pointe Marianne Estate, in receiving the Officers and Crew (26 in number) of the *Teviotdale*, a large iron vessel burnt at sea about 80 miles South West of Diego Garcia on the 1st November 1876, and who arrived at Pointe Marianne on the 4th of the same month. During their stay at Pointe Marianne, which last 49 days, twenty three of them were entertained to the best of Mr. Desjardins' power; the three others were kindly received by Mr D'Antoine at Minni-Minni. It is also due to Mr. Spurs, of East Point Estate, to mention that he offered his services to the Captain of the wrecked ship and sent some provisions to aid in supporting the crew.'

Ackroyd mentions too that he talked to the *Teviotdale*'s captain, as they both returned to Mauritius aboard the *Barso*, the schooner which at that time was one of the regular supply ships to some of the Chagos Islands. In our book, *Chagos: A History*, which I hope will come out in a very few months' time. I have the following paragraph, in a chapter devoted to a number of wrecks involving the Chagos (and several lots of survivors reaching the islands):

Then, on 1 November 1876, the British barque *Teviotdale* caught fire 80 miles south-west of Diego Garcia, and was abandoned. Her crew of 26 succeeded in reaching the island after three days, and spent some weeks at Pointe Marianne. [footnote 7, see below]. The *Teviotdale* had been carrying a cargo of coal from Dundee to Bombay, India. Some ten months later, on 17 September 1877, according to a report which subsequently appeared in the *Daily News*, the Peninsular and Oriental (P&O)

mail steamer *Hindostan*, approaching Aden from China, boarded an abandoned vessel which was completely gutted, with coal still smouldering in her hold. She was identified as the *Teviotdale*, of Glasgow, by the official number and registered tonnage marked on the main-hatch beam. An extraordinary last journey for this iron vessel!

her two other boats never reached land. The crew stayed at Six Islands until they were picked up two-and-a-half months later by the plantation's supply vessel, the brig *Ibis* (Captain J.L.R. Dolphin) and taken to Mauritius.[6]

Then, on 1 November 1876, the British barque *Teviotdale* caught fire 80 miles south-west of Diego Garcia, and was abandoned. Her crew of 26 succeeded in reaching the island after three days, and spent some weeks at Pointe Marianne.[7] The *Teviotdale* had been carrying a cargo of coal from Dundee to India. Some ten months later, on 17 September 1877, according to a report which subsequently appeared in the *Daily News*, the Peninsular and Oriental mail steamer *Hindostan*, approaching Aden from China, boarded an abandoned vessel which was completely gutted, with coal still smouldering in her hold. She was identified as the *Teviotdale*, of Glasgow, by the official number and registered tonnage marked on the main-hatch beam. An extraordinary last journey for this iron vessel!

Whalers: snippets from the log books

In the mid-19th century, as Special Magistrate Anderson had reported in 1838

East Point plantation circa 1886. Photo by unknown passenger aboard visiting P & O liner (NW-S collection).

7 T NA CO 167/573 J. Ackroyd, Report dated 26 January 1877. The *Teviotdale* was a barque launched in 1869 and closely resembling the well-known *Cutty Sark*. As this book goes to press, Stuart Jenkins, a descendant [grandson] of one of the vessel's crew, George Jenkins, is engaged in editing his forebear's diary of the accident and his sojourn in Diego Garcia.

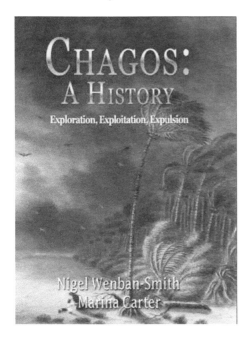

Diego Garcia and Nigel Wenban-Smith

Nigel's book, *Chagos: Exploration, Exploitation, Expulsion*. By Nigel Wenban-Smith and Dr Marina Carter. In the book, there are several nuggets of information from Chapter 9:

Witness to Neptune's Moods

Teviotdale

East Point photo

Ackroyd (Notes to Chapter 9)

About Nigel Wenban-Smith

Relevant career: Nigel, born 1936, educated at King's College Cambridge and served his National Service in the Royal Navy. After National Service he joined the Civil Service. A former British diplomat, Nigel was Assistant Principal of the Commonwealth Relations Office 1960-1961 for the British Government, now the Foreign and Commonwealth Office (FCO). In retirement he served as Chairman of the Friends of the Chagos Islands Association.

Notes to Chapter 9

1 Wilmer and Smith's *European Times*, 7 June 1859.

2 *Commercial Gazette* 23 July 1859.

3 NA CO 167/489 Report of Mauritius Marine Board hearing on 9 May 1866.

4 After the crew had departed, the *Shannon* must have been scavenged thoroughly; the deckhouse, for example, was re-erected in front of the Pointe Marianne manager's house, where, ten years later, it served as the establishment's dispensary.

5 TNA CO 167/445. Letter from Board of Trade to CO, dated 3 October 1862, enclosing report from Port Louis Shipping Master.

6 TNA CO 167/530. Letter dated 2 March 1870 from John Lothrop Motley, Head of the US Legation, London, to the Foreign Secretary (eventually forwarded to Port Louis from Board of Trade). The details of the ship and the photograph are from Whidden, J.D. *Ocean Life in the Old Sailing Ship Days: from forecastle to quarter-deck*, Little, Brown & Co, 1908, pp. 185–6.

7 TNA CO 167/573 J. Ackroyd, Report dated 26 January 1877. The *Teviotdale* was a barque launched in 1869 and closely resembled the well-known *Cutty Sark*, launched the same year. As this book goes to press, Stewart Jenkins, grandson of one of the vessel's crew, George Jenkins, is engaged in editing his forebear's diary of the accident and his sojourn in Diego Garcia.

8 Scott writes that 'during the 1860s and 1870s ... and for a decade or so before and after, the seas around Diego Garcia were a favoured haunt of whalers, with some wrecked on its reefs'. Scott, R. *Limuria: the Lesser Dependencies of Mauritius*, OUP, 1961 [reprinted 1976 Greenwood, USA] p. 259.

9 Among the vessels whose logs are preserved in the New Bedford and Kendall Whaling Museums, the *Herald* (1834), *Tuskadora* (1840), *Harbinger* (1846), *Hector* (1846), *Montezuma* (1848) and *Merlin* (1870)

Nigel Wenban-Smith's career in the British Diplomatic Service included a spell as Commissioner for the British Indian Ocean Territory in the early 1980s. This sparked his interest in the conservation of the Chagos Archipelago, which led to his involvement, after retirement, in the Friends of the Chagos (now the Chagos Conservation Trust), including six years as its Chairman. Over the past decade he has turned his attention increasingly to the archipelago's little-known history.

Nigel's co-author, Dr Marina Carter

Dr Marina Carter trained as a historian, and holds a doctorate from the University of Oxford. She is currently a member of an AHRC-funded research team working on historical labour diasporas in the Indian Ocean and is based at the University of Edinburgh and in London. She wrote her thesis on 19th century Indian migration to Mauritius and has specialist knowledge of the South West Indian Ocean islands. Outside the academic field Dr Carter has worked as a history and heritage consultant on a number of projects, including for the Mauritius Museums Council, and is a regular contributor to the Dictionary of Mauritian Biography. She authored several chapters for the Insight *Guide to Mauritius, Reunion and Seychelles*, and the Indian Ocean entries to the *Encyclopaedia of the Indian Diaspora*.

Their book *Chagos: A History: Exploration, Exploitation, Expulsion*. can be purchased from: https://www.ypdbooks.com/non-fiction/1532-chagos-a-history-exploration-exploitation-expulsion-YPD01728.html Telephone: 01904 431 213.

Today, Diego Garcia and the other 60 small islands of the Chagos Archipelago are a militarised area owned by the United Kingdom and administered by the UK as the British Indian Ocean Territory (BIOT). The UK government represents the territory internationally. Diego Garcia is the largest of the islands in the archipelago and is the only inhabited island. The population is mainly composed of military personnel along with some civilians in supporting roles. Through a UK/US agreement, parts of Diego Garcia are used by the United States military for activities in the region and the number of personnel on the base varies from time to time but is often in excess of 1,000 staff. As a protected marine and land environment, all consumable food and equipment are brought to Diego Garcia by sea or air, and all non-biodegradable waste is shipped off the island as well.

Historically speaking, Diego Garcia has always been a strategically important staging point for both civilian and military purposes, and as such is identified as an ETOPS (Extended Range Twin Engine Operations) emergency landing site (en-route alternate) for flight planning purposes of commercial airliners. This allows twin-engine commercial aircraft (such as the Airbus A330, Boeing 767 or Boeing 777) to make theoretical non-stop flights between city pairs such as Perth and Dubai (9,013.61 km or 5,600.80 miles), Hong Kong and Johannesburg (10,658 km or 6,623 miles) or Singapore and São Paulo (15,985.41 km or 9,932.87 miles), all while maintaining a suitable diversion airport within 180 minutes' flying time with one engine inoperable.

Space Shuttle – The island was one of 33 emergency landing sites worldwide for the NASA Space Shuttle. None of these facilities was ever used throughout the life of the shuttle programme.

Chapter Five

Dysart – Quality Street

My grandfather's seafaring days came to an end in 1884 when he became a Customs House Officer based in Dundee. During this period, he had met and married his wife, Elizabeth McEwan, and had started a family, living at 37 Gellatly Street, Dundee.

After their first four children were born, Georgina followed by Grace, Louise and James, George was promoted to become the Customs Officer at the small port of Dysart, located on the north coast of the Forth Estuary in the County of Fife.

Dysart once had a Customs House to deal with smuggled contraband coming in through the harbour. In those days it was tobacco and spirits which the officers dealt with and those found smuggling were sent to Cupar to de dealt with.

In 1904, Mr George Jenkins was promoted from Principal Officer to Superintendent, having served for eight years. At the same time, the staff was increased by the addition of a second officer, Mr John Hill, who came from Burntisland. In the photograph of the two men in the doorway to the Mercantile Marine Office, Mr Jenkins is on the left. The office was in Mid Quality Street.

At that time, Dysart was a small coal mining town busy exporting coal to Scandinavia. My father, Charles Henry Ward, was born there in 1896, followed by my Uncle Frederick (Freddie) in 1900 to complete the family.

The family started their life in Dysart living above the Mercantile Marine Office (photo on previous page) in Mid Quality Street, now called simply Quality Street (photo below).

Dysart – Pan Ha'

Later the family moved down to The Tide Waiter's House, also known as the Customs House, in Hie Gait, (now called Number 9) located on the Pan Ha' very close to the beach.

I suspect that this move was necessary due to the accommodation provided above the Custom House Office being inadequate to house the whole family.

During their time in Dysart the family suffered the sad loss of Georgina who died of consumption at the young age of 22. Georgina had been born in 1881 and died in 1903; she was buried in Dysart Cemetery. Subsequently, Elizabeth McEwan, George's wife, who died in 1918, aged 63, was buried there in 1922. In 1973 my father Charles Jenkins died, aged 77; he too was buried in the family plot.

It is interesting to note that during his life-time my father, nor any of my surviving uncles or aunts, ever mentioned the Mid Quality Street address in Dysart.

When my father first took me to Dysart in 1951, he only took me to what he called the Customs House in the Pan Ha' on the corner of the Hie Gait cobbled alleyway (The Tide Waiter's House, 9 Hie Gait).

At this time, the whole of the Pan Ha' area was in a very sad state of run-down dereliction, although the coal mine situated above the town was still in full production with an ugly slag heap located a little way eastward along the beach.

I also remember that the beach was largely covered in rounded coal pebbles. Locals used to take their carts down to the beach and scavenge for fuel, as can be seen in the photograph dated c.1955.

The Customs House (Tide Waiter's House)

My father and I found that the front door to the Pan Ha' house was unlocked and he took me inside. I found it interesting that the steps up to the front door were matched inside by steps down to a relatively large ground floor room, the surface of which was made up of compacted earth. The whole place smelt of damp and decay and had obviously been in this state for some time. Stairs led up to the upper floors and I do not remember noticing any kitchen facilities. We did not stay long in the house and on the way out father noticed that the front door knocker was still in place in a very dirty state. It was obvious that the knocker brought back the memory of his mother vigorously keeping it brightly polished. He asked me to get a screwdriver from the car so that he could unscrew the knocker from the door. The knocker was in a very poor condition; it had been polished so much over many years that holes had been worn through its brass surface in several places.

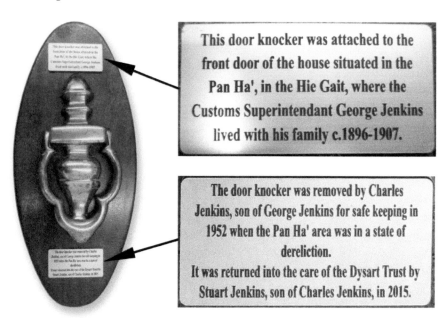

This door knocker was attached to the front door of the house situated in the Pan Ha', in the Hie Gait, where the Customs Superintendant George Jenkins lived with his family c.1896-1907.

The door knocker was removed by Charles Jenkins, son of George Jenkins for safe keeping in 1952 when the Pan Ha' area was in a state of dereliction.
It was returned into the care of the Dysart Trust by Stuart Jenkins, son of Charles Jenkins, in 2015.

Dysart Customs House Door-Knocker - c1896

On our return home to Hoddesdon in Hertfordshire, it was carefully repaired by my brother Sandy (Alexander), re-polished and mounted on a mahogany plaque to enable it to be hung on the wall.

The Pan Ha' house door knocker was then passed on to my Aunt Louise and afterwards it was looked after by her daughter Clare until her death in 2014. In 2015 it was returned to the Dysart Trust.

All that remains today of the Dysart coalmining industry in the area is the Frances Colliery Pithead to the north-east side of Dysart. This is the only remnant of a once thriving and lucrative coal mining industry.

Later, my grandfather became the Customs Superintendent for the Port of Alloa, which was then the largest and busiest port in Scotland, and the family moved to the Customs House there.

George Jenkins was then a notable member of society and it was during this period that he gave his *Teviotdale* voyage lecture at the nearby Tullibody Public Hall in 1909.

Alloa

Alloa had a thriving port in medieval times, long before written records, right up till its closure in 1970.

Customs House Officers await the arrival of a steam ship at Alloa Port

In the background, two sailing vessels can be seen in front of the industrial area.

Visiting Alloa today you will find memorial stone plaques at the place where the port was situated. Inscriptions tell of the importance of the place in its heyday. An example of three of the stone plaques can be found amongst the remains of the quayside foundations which relay stories of its past history.

The importance maritime trade to all corners of the globe from of Alloa is clear to see, since Daniel Defoe wrote in 1723, "At Alloa … A Merchant May Trade To All Parts Of The World …'

Long before this, the geography and geology of the natural surroundings meant that at this point in the estuary, a safe landing could be had under various conditions. The earliest record of an anchorage at Alloa is 1502.

Increasing trade and prosperity in the area meant that the town was thriving and growing. Alloa was the chief town of Clackmannanshire and to celebrate the growth of the town, Lime Tree Walk to the harbour was planted with rows of limes in 1714.

Today, rows of lime trees still line both carriageways, re-planted in 2008. James Erskine, Earl of Mar and Kellie, commented: "Now that I am assured that there will be a double row of lime trees, I am very pleased that the Lime Tree Walk will once again become a distinctive and historic part of Alloa, connecting the town centre and its former port. Ultimately, I am very glad that the address 'The Shore, Alloa' is returning to be a dignified rather than derelict part of the town."

The Jenkins family lived in Alloa until after WW1. Later, after the death of his wife, he married again and lived the remainder of his life in Dundee. The rest of the family then all went their own separate ways.

Acknowledgements and Contributors

George Jenkins (Original diary of adventures)
Charles Jenkins (Family history documents)
Stuart Jenkins (Research & editing)
Melanie Grace (Research & editing)

Robert Hughes (Photography, design layout, maps, research & editing)
Carol McNeill (Introduction, proofreading & editing)
Terence Crump (The Cottage Studio – Mapping design)

Thanks to Eilleen and George Taylor of Shinfield History Society for transcribing documents written in Old English script handwriting into modern text. Thanks also to Kirstine Hughes for her typing skills in the early stages of the book.

Special thanks to Chris Calder, Chairperson of Tullibody History Group for providing the photo 'Public Hall, Tullibody c.1909'.

Photo by David Smith on page 142. Source: Wikimedia Commons, http://www.geograph.org.uk/profile/5465 David Smith.

To read more about Chris and the Tullibody History group visit www.tullibodyhistorygroup.com

Photo Credits

Howard Birchmore: pp. 4-5, 37, 38, 42, 44-45, 47, 48-49, 59, 60, 62-63, 74, 75, 80, 142

Terence Crump: pp. 50, 65, 72, 112, 114

Dysart Trust: pp. 11, 127, 128, 129, 130

Robert Hughes: pp. 34, 84, 105, 113, 132, 133, 135, 136, 137, 141

Dr Andrew Jeffrey: p. 147

Jenkins Archive: pp. 12, 27, 30, 83, 130, 134

National Maritime Museum: pp. 22-24, 140, 141

Brian Phillips: pp. 33, 61

Bob Scarlett: pp. 99-103

David Smith: p. 144

D. R. Stoddart: p. 119

Tullibody History Group: p. 27

Unknown passenger: p. 122

Nigel Wenban-Smith: p. 123

Appendix 1

About the Teviotdale

Discovering the Sail and Rigging Plan for the *Teviotdale*

A stroke of luck and a miraculous find saw the discovery of the original Sail and Rigging Plan for the *Teviotdale* along with numerous other plans from the Barclay, Curle and Co shipyard at Stobcross. Some decades ago, a keen-eyed person came across a rather sad looking sight, a derelict coal-shed with bundles of ships' plans, neglected, damp and water-stained. With the roof about to collapse and all these documents lost, the person in question rescued a whole host of valuable and historic original plans from Barclay's ship-building yard on the banks of the Clyde. It turns out, that amongst these plans was the Sail and Rigging Plan for the *Teviotdale* of 1869. The documents were transmitted to the National Maritime Museum of London, and on to the Memorial University of Newfoundland for safe-keeping and archive.

The damp and coal-stained original Rigging Plans for the *Teviotdale* are shown here, and below a repaired version along with some relevant data on the ship.

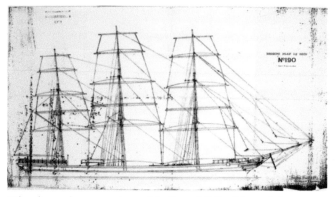

Rigging plan courtesy National Maritime Museum.

140

Teviotdale

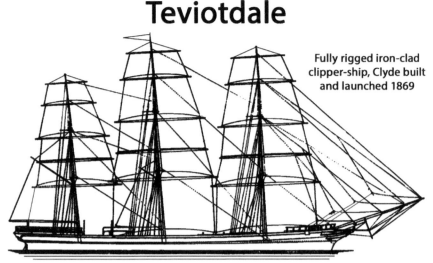

Fully rigged iron-clad clipper-ship, Clyde built and launched 1869

Shipbuilders & Engineers: Barclay Curle & Company, Glasgow, Scotland, UK.

Ship: Sail, 3 mast, iron-clad, fully rigged. Gross weight: 1259 ton registered. Launched: Friday 9th July 1869. Length: 227.8ft. Beam: 36.15ft. Draught: 22.05ft. Mast (main) 148ft. Crew: 26. Cargo: 1800t general (coal).

www.ClippershipTeviotdale1876.co.uk

Ship-builder of the *Teviotdale*

Barclay Curle & Co were the shipbuilder of the *Teviotdale*; she was built for the United Kingdom to India trade route.

Barclay, Curle and Co was a major Scottish shipbuilder situated on the north bank of the Clyde in Glasgow.

The *Teviotdale* was launched on 9th July 1869.

Barclay Curle & Co also built many other sea-going vessels; clipper ships, barques and other fine vessels for a wide range of trades such as cargo, passenger, ferries and coasters. Their methods of propulsion were initially by sail, but during the late 19th century they increasingly built paddle steamers and screw steamers.

The shipbuilding business of Barclay Curle and Company was founded by John Barclay at Whiteinch on the Clyde bank, Glasgow in 1818. John Barclay's son Robert took Robert Curle and James Hamilton into partnership in 1845 and the name changed to Robert Barclay and Curle. In 1847 John Fergusson was admitted as a partner. 1852 saw the first ships being built in iron. By 1857 the business had begun to manufacture marine engines; two other partners were added in the same year, Andrew Maclean and Archibald Gilchrist.

Nearby, a large engineering works was built at Stobcross in 1862. In the following year Robert Barclay died and the name was changed to Barclay, Curle and Company to reflect this. By 1869, the yards had built 32 full-rigged ships, 2 barques and 1 schooner. The Stobcross yard alone had made 22 sailing ships. In 1876, Barclay Curle and Company moved their yard downriver from Stobcross just opposite Linthouse, near the recently failed yard of Wingates.

During the 1880s Barclay, Curle and Co had built its first steel steamer. In 1912 they acquired the Elderslie Shipyard and graving dock of John Shearer & Sons to assist with orders at the Clydeholm Yard in Whiteinch. Also during 1912, Swan, Hunter and Wigham Richardson took over Barclay Curle and Company Limited which became a trading subsidiary, including all its yards and docks. It's interesting to note that in 1851 there were six ship-building yards on the Clyde, by 1900 there were around 20.

Resources (Barclay Curle) used: https://www.gracesguide.co.uk/Barclay,_Curle_and_Co

Resources (*Teviotdale*) used: http://www.clydeships.co.uk and search for *Teviotdale*, 60444.

Teviotdale's Maiden Voyage

On 11th August, 1869 she sailed from Glasgow for Bombay – this was her maiden voyage. Most of her subsequent voyages were to India, St Lawrence, Canada, New Zealand or Australia. Records show of one single 'emigrant' voyage to Australia, under the guidance of Captain Nicol, where she sailed from Glasgow on 17th February 1873. She was recorded to have left the Clyde on 21st February, passed Tukar (unknown), and arrived in Melbourne, Australia on 22nd May 1873. On board were just 15 passengers, of which one died on board; in very heavy gales off the Portuguese coast, the longboat was destroyed and one crew member was washed away.

The Barclay Curle & Co Shipyard

Barclay Curle Shipbuilders and Titan crane. Stobcross, (Clydebank) Glasgow.

Photo: David Smith.

The Barclay Curle Shipyard still exists today; likewise, a large structure on the site is present, sadly the yard does not make world-class ships any more. The site is littered with enormous piles of mangled scrap iron and steel, though the massive 'Titan Crane' remains to this day as a testament to the importance of these ship-building businesses and a reminder of their heyday.

If you have any information about the *Teviotdale* 1876 clipper ship that you think we may be interested to hear about or include on our website, please contact us.

We would be delighted to hear from any descendants of crew-members who were on board the ship during its final, or any of its previous voyages. She had two captains over her short life

144

that we know of: Captain Nicol (officially logged at Wellington NZ, 26th August 1875) and Captain Robert Jones who set sail on 26th July 1876 from Camperdown Dock, Dundee. His was to be the fateful and final voyage of the *Teviotdale* during which the ship was abandoned due to uncontrollable fire on board.

Help! We are also looking for your help in locating the descendants of a Scottish artist by the name of A. R. Blair. He may have been a professional artist or indeed an amateur working is his spare time. Blair was probably from Tullibody or Alloa in Clackmannanshire, Scotland. Blair was commissioned by George Jenkins to create a series of pictures to show the final voyage and adventures of the *Teviotdale* in 1876. The pictures that Blair produced depicted various aspects of life on board the three-masted clipper ship during its passage around the world. We know George Jenkins visited London to have 'lantern slides' created from them and George subsequently used these slides to give an illustrated talk to a packed audience in the Tullibody Public Hall on 18*th* December 1909.

We are also trying to track down the whereabouts of an original painting of the *Teviotdale* in 1872 by the Scottish artist Samuel H Fyfe. There is evidence to show such a painting exists and it appears to be in the hands of a private collector. The painting will show a three-masted sailing ship, much like the clipper ship *Cutty Sark*, also built in 1869. Please contact us if you can shed any light on this work of art. The painting may be in Scotland or perhaps even further afield, who knows?

Maritime experiences

For many of us our ocean experience is that of a ferry-crossing, a yachting holiday or time spent on a cruise ship. Rarely do we experience really bad weather, let alone perilous or life-threatening conditions as can be found in the great oceans. It is times like these that the sailor or merchant seaman earns his 'salt' or worth. We rely on professional sailors, skippers and masters with their experience, knowledge and skills to navigate vessels loaded with passengers and cargo a safe passage through stormy waters and into port.

The Unfinished Final Voyage?

For her final voyage, the *Teviotdale* was carrying coal to Bombay. We can only guess what she may have brought back from there. It could possibly be jute, flax or linen as there was a large amount of industry in Dundee processing these raw materials into woven materials for worldwide consumption.

E&OE. We have undertaken a great deal of research in the re-construction of the story of the *Teviotdale*. Most of the evidence has been gained from old original documents, official copies of certain documents, copies of old newspaper articles and old photographs both from within the family and received from contributors. We hope and believe that all the information within the *Teviotdale* clipper ship website is true and accurate. If, however, you have any corrections or information about the *Teviotdale* clipper ship of 1876 (launched in1869) or any of its 27 crew members, we would be pleased to hear from you. Please contact Stuart Jenkins via the *Teviotdale* website at www.clippershipteviotdale1876.co.uk.

Appendix 2

SS Dalhousie

George Jenkins' father was drowned at sea along with 33 other lives, when the SS *Dalhousie* went down in the Tay during a gale force storm in November 1864. George Jenkins would have only been eight years old.

Evening Telegraph (Thursday 15th August 2013) – Article by Dr Andrew Jeffrey (Historian)

Unlike tragedies such as the loss of the lifeboat *Mona* or the Tay Bridge disaster, what befell the steam ship *Dalhousie* has been forgotten, despite the death of 34 men, women and children.

Now, Dundee historian Dr Andrew Jeffrey is shedding new light on the story of a ship that sailed into oblivion during a howling storm – in the hands of a captain with a less than stellar reputation.

The SS *Dalhousie*, described at the time as a 'rakish-looking little steamer', was built in 1861 by the Gourlay Brothers & Co in Dundee for the Dundee-Newcastle run. (Vessel number 29453, yard number 10, passenger cargo, iron screw steamer.)

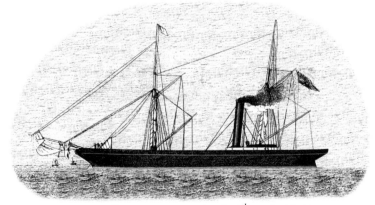

SS Dalhousie, Launched: 9th Feb 1861
Image: Dr Andrew Jeffrey

Early in its career, however, the ship's captain, Henry K. Glenny came to the attention of his employers for all the wrong reasons – running the ship aground while trying to enter Arbroath. Despite this black mark, the *Dalhousie* made the Newcastle route a success until the night of November 24th 1864. She was heading back to Dundee and was battling a force nine gale from the east.

Many of the passengers, especially the women and children, cowered in the ship's saloon as the wind whipped through the rigging and the ship lurched against the sea. But the battering was too much and the *Dalhousie*'s engines failed. "Given the sea conditions, once the ship had broken down almost nothing could have saved her," says Dr Jeffrey. Pushed towards the shore and probably broadside on to the raging sea, she was doomed.

"Just before midnight there were reports of a distress signal south of the Tay channel, and distress rockets and two guns had also been heard. Concerns were raised, but, somewhat controversially, the St Andrews lifeboat refused to go out to sea due to the gale."

The following day, a shipping agent named Inglis travelled to Tentsmuir to see what had befallen the *Dalhousie* – perhaps she was simply aground?

Mr Inglis was met by a cart containing two bodies that had been found by local people and the mystery was solved. *Dalhousie* was down in 30ft of water with only her masts showing. "Inglis identified the bodies as Captain Glenny and Tom Bisset, a ship's engineer, from Broughty Ferry," said Dr Jeffrey.

"By then, wreckage and bodies were strewn along much of Tentsmuir Beach." Not one of the passengers or crew survived. A few days later, a diver went down and, in the saloon, he saw the bodies of two children, both girls, huddled together. "A woman's body could be seen jammed behind the stove, a small boy held tightly in her arms." As bodies were brought up to the support vessel, the tug *Rob Roy*, there was another grim twist. When the body of the woman trapped behind the stove reached the surface, the engineer of the *Rob Roy* collapsed – it was his wife and he didn't even know she had been aboard *Dalhousie*.

Captain Glenny lies in Dundee's Western Cemetery. Some other bodies were never recovered. In the weeks following, a public appeal collected £3,000 for the 18 women left widowed and the 52 children orphaned by the disaster.

See www.eveningtelegraph.co.uk/2016/01/13/dalhousie-the-tay-shipwreck-you-may-not-have-heard-about/

More can be found about the SS *Dalhousie* by visiting: www.clydeships.co.uk.

PRINTED AND BOUND BY:

Copytech (UK) Limited trading as Printondemand-worldwide,
9 Culley Court, Bakewell Road, Orton Southgate.
Peterborough, PE2 6XD, United Kingdom.